Praise for Environmental

Sometimes whimsical and funny, sometimes : always stirring. They insist on engaging the re. sense and psyche…This book has the power to transform.
—Rabbi Avram Davis, Ph.D.

If mind pollution is the worst kind, if the most basic environmental reforms need to be made in human thinking, *then Michael Tobias's* Environmental Meditation *points the way toward hope.*
—Roderick Frazier Nash, Professor of History and Environmental Studies, University of California, Santa Barbara

Superb writing from a soaringly powerful mind, Tobias' book…builds numberless bridges between East and West, feeling and thought, poetry and the hard fact, the self and the world, the Earth and mankind. …Tobias weaves a vast visionary tapestry of luminous connections which speak with equal force to the soul in private meditation and to the self in search of meaningful action.
—Sophia S. Morgan, Comparative Literature, Ph.D.

With language as lush as a tropical forest, and insight clear as the high mountain air, Michael Tobias depicts perfect moments at the embrace between the natural and the human.
—David Rothenberg, author, *Hand's End* and *Is It Painful To Think?*

ENVIRONMENTAL
MEDITATION

Other Works by Michael Tobias

Literary

World War III: Population and Biology at the End of the Millennium; A Vision of Nature: Traces of the Original World; Mahavira; Rage & Reason; Life Force: The World of Jainism; Fatal Exposure; Voice of the Planet; Mountain People (ed.); After Eden: History, Ecology & Conscience; Deep Ecology (ed.); Deva; The Mountain Spirit (ed.); Believe (with William Shatner); The Autobiography of a Boy; Tsa; Dhaulagirideon; The Immortality Trilogy; Vermeer; Harry & Arthur

Films & Television Series

A Day in the Life of Ireland; Voice of the Planet (ten hours); Black Tide; Ahimsa: Nonviolence; Antarctica: The Last Continent; Ozone Crisis; Animal Rights; The Gift; Space Futures; Sand and Lightning; Cloudwalker; Kazantzakis; The Sixth Annual Genesis Awards; The Fifth Annual Genesis Awards; Science Notes (thirty-two parts); The Making of Voice of the Planet; The Power Game (four hours)

ENVIRONMENTAL MEDITATION

by Michael Tobias

The Crossing Press
Freedom, CA 95019

Cover and book design by Sheryl Karas
Cover photo by Michael Tobias

Printed in the U.S.A.

Library of Congress Cataloging-in Publication Data

Tobias, Michael.
    Environmental meditation / by Michael Tobias.
        p. cm.
    Includes bibliographical references.
    ISBN 0-89594-586-X.--ISBN 0-89594-585-1 (pbk.)
    1. Human ecology--Religious aspects--Meditations.
    2. Man (Theology)--Meditations. I. Title
BL624.T625 1993
179'.1--dc20   93-5276
                                      CIP

Dedicated to
Jane Morrison Tobias
with Love

Table of Contents

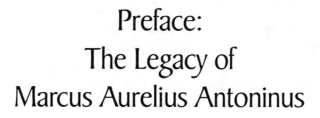

Preface:
The Legacy of
Marcus Aurelius Antoninus

*The Ox Mountain was stripped utterly bare. And the people, seeing it
stripped utterly bare, think the Ox Mountain never had
any woods on it at all.*

—Mencius, as quoted by Thomas Merton[1]

When I first decided to couple the meditation genre with that of the environment, I was concerned that the outcome might suffer from a certain trendiness of deep breaths; or, conversely, be excessively weighed down by those many dark nights of the soul with which ecology is rightfully preoccupied.

We are assaulted daily by contradictions that offer no obvious solution. Indeed, there *are* no solutions to some things. Darkness, for example. Who ever said darkness needed a solution in the first place? The darkness of night, the darkness of evil? The spheres of darkness are protean, like animal suffering, human disparities or the evident brutalities of evolution. Both Buddha and Darwin attempted to understand these glaring truths about the world, but neither were prepared to offer vacuous solutions.

I have begun this volume in the grey tones of impinging darkness, very much concerned about the stifling problems that agitate the contemporary world we inhabit. In contemplating these crises, I have sought mental remedies through mental process; amelioration through philosophy; tranquility that should follow from immersion in thought, in the web of connections whose most predictable and fruitful link is the eternal self, an ecological self. A self that is accessible, inviolate and filled with promise.

The reader will find nothing to follow, per se, in the present volume. There are certain guided visualizations and logical arguments, but no formula. No pretense to solving the world's pain or unlocking its pleasure. The writing of these essays has been its own form of meditation. A gentle, meandering view of myself in the world, without pre-conception or goal; clinging to no one theory or maxim, prepared to surprise myself, to be carried away or stopped short. And as such, a confessional and inquisitive technique that has helped me to get through each day, and which I can thus safely recommend to others. From darkness to light, each of the following meditations takes the reader up a ladder, higher and higher, toward a psychological release.

Release is key to the contemplative knot our times have woven and it is the essence of the process set forth in this book.

"Ask, and it shall be given you; seek, and ye shall find; knock and it shall be opened unto you." From the time that St. Matthew uttered these words, the inner life has perpetually voiced such hopes and comforts. Solutions already in place, in a state of nature, a state of theological grace. According to this premise, meditation was the means of untying those knots, of opening a letter from God addressed to one's innermost being. "He Himself is discovered within myself, resplendent in the interior of my miserable heart" wrote St. Symeon.[2]

The comforts of meditation and the sanctity it presupposes are, of course, increasingly unsure. There was a time when Jews and Christians were martyred for a cause. Today, all of nature is martyred, and with it, most reasonable thought—for no cause at all!

Doubts and grimaces are thriving as ethical whiplash unleashes new rules of the evolutionary game. Strategy and counter-strategy, disease, war, toxic nightmares and the breakdown of nearly every ecosystem coincide with an amazing human capacity for hope and celebration, even on the very brink of calamity.

In the heart of the human disaster, there is Nature, alright. Beyond the easy categories and the escape to national parks. Beyond the very nature of pessimism and despair. The idea of nature combines the least certainty with the greatest hope, maximizing one's ignorance in the face of unabashed exuberance. Ignorance of the overwhelming impact our species is wreaking on the planet. Exuberance which is our nature. These predicates all hinge on the flimsily construed Self, a quantum of restless consciousness which creates new nature every day. Nature inside us, all around us. The mind and the heart create the world for themselves. Starting perpetually fresh. Stimulated by the promise of deliverance. Of release.

This mental and emotional nature—this human nature—presents every solution and every problem, and this undifferentiated abundance does not make the task any easier for a curious or tormented mind. Mind in nature is, in fact, the worst sort of redundancy, tautology or equivalency. Mind in nature is pure paradox. "I Am that I Am" writes the poet of *Exodus* (iii, 14).

"General truths, which at the same time bear the character of an inward necessity, must be independent of experience—clear and certain by themselves. They are therefore called knowledge *a priori*," Kant says in the very first page of his own monumental meditation, *Critique Of Pure Reason*.

There was a time, not too long ago, when reasonable men and women expected reasonable truths, and believed with all the power of their intellect and hearts that those truths had an *a priori* basis in nature. Those same truths—Kant's "inward necessity"—are still with us. Men and women still believe.

Belief is lovely. But belief in what? The world has become less and less reasonable. As the ecological onslaught intensifies, the fateful words of William Butler Yeats, from his poem "The Second Coming" come back to haunt the whole person:

> "Things fall apart; the centre cannot hold;
> Mere anarchy is loosed upon the world,
> The blood-dimmed tide is loosed, and everywhere
> The ceremony of innocence is drowned;
> The best lack all conviction, while the worst
> Are full of passionate intensity."

Somewhere between the pensées of Marcus Aurelius, the traumatic caveats of Yeats and the deep breaths of yogic practice, the concept of meditation has taken a firm hold on the imagination, connoting that process by which a truth—"true consciousness"—is discovered. A new country of the mind. That past which had been lost or obscured. The future which is blind and in need.

Emperor Marcus Aurelius (121-178 A.D.) was a man who lived much of his life in a state of quiet contemplation, and Rome was the lucky beneficiary of his spirit. He believed in virtue, in the simplicity of life, in piety and benevolence, modesty and patience, and these qualities were the subject of his literary and political conscience. He stands out in my mind as one who evidently discovered the secret of true meditation. What he accomplished during his lifetime was significant. Marcus Aurelius summed up his age in *The Meditations*, written from a battlefield, soliciting inner directives and illuminations, seeking strength and renewal from within in order to resolve outer conflict. He was partially successful and his life reads like his open book, a struggle with contraries, a beacon shrouded in ineluctable cloud; metaphors often too noble for the times in which he lived.

In Japan, the Shogun Ashikaga Yoshimasa similarly strove toward equanimity during the late 1400's, at the height of Kyoto's horrible Onin Civil War, by abdicating politics in favor of an aesthetic, meditative lifestyle which he tried to promote for the common man, and not without some success.

After all the war embers had died out—both in Rome and in Kyoto—the world remembers the ascetic, Marcus Aurelius and the ex-Shogun, tea celebrant, Yoshimasa.

The meditation has no beginning and no end. Like the medieval philosopher's definition of God, the Self fashions endless mental itineraries in its quest to return home, to leave home, to make that journey from consternation and nervous angst to confidence and unfaltering joy. The process of meditation, however intellectual, must ultimately affect the heart. The head stands lord and ruler over contradiction and dialectic. The heart, however, engenders the feelings that can successfully address the needs of humanity and all other life forms. Working in respectful tandem, the head and the heart constitute a wondrous fellowship, an original, untainted compliance with greater laws, the forces of nature of which we are but a humble part.

By such meditation, whatever the circumstances, the individual has confessed to a deep reflection normally absent during the consuming rigors of daily life. Every human being has the power, the inner eye, to meditate.

As a noun, *meditation* celebrates an access to revelation which is supremely personal. As an intransitive verb, with no specific direct object, *meditate* reaches toward a generous underground of the Self, something that hints, variously, of Buddhistic pantheism or eternal concentration. As a transitive verb, oriented towards accomplishment, it invokes the intellectual or emotional hub where moral therapy, physical healing, the perception of beauty and conflict resolution can reach new heights.

In short, it is a word that strives inwardly toward the best we are or can be. A word charged with great dreams, fervent hopes and fantastic discoveries.

By *environmental meditation*, then, I have attempted to react to exasperating contradictions, desires and nightmares in our time, with reasonable hopes and reasonable doubts; to explore my own inner feelings under siege, and, by analogy, to examine the collective psyche as it approaches the end of a very difficult and spectacular millennium. How do generous and thoughtful people cope with ecological distress and seemingly insoluble problems? When our pastimes, sensibilities or sense of justice and purity are threatened, what are our mental options? How do we deal with ecological disappointment and sadness? We have grown up living with every compromise. At what point do we say "No," or roll up our sleeves and fight? When do we retreat? And to where? Who are we fighting and what is there to win? A species, saved from extinction, when all species are threatened? A child, spared from hunger, when a million other children will die? Is it enough to simply vote, to console ourselves with the two-bit wisdom that while the Earth is perfect, mankind seems almost incapable of living up to it?

Conversely, what wellsprings of aesthetic calm, historical and poetic precedents, what spiritual antidotes are immemorially present in the meditative Self to counter the weight of environmental troubles confronting *Homo sapiens* today? What are the possibilities for happiness in an age of ecological collapse?

Finally, how might meditation on the very idea of nature revolutionize the struggling Self and regain the original blessings of Being in this world? This emphasis on the attainment of happiness concerns the second half of this volume.

In joy, as in anxiety, these are some of the absorptions with which this work modestly dwells.

—*Michael Tobias*
Santa Fe & Santa Monica, Summer of 1992

[1] *In Thomas Merton,* Mystics and Zen Masters, *p. 67, Farrar, Straus & Giroux, NY, 1967.*
[2] *See* Caesar and Christ—A History of Roman Civilization and of Christianity from their Beginnings to A.D. 325, *by Will Durant, pp. 422-432, Simon and Schuster, NY, 1944.*

I
On the Relationship Between Country and City

All I ask is good lands and a spacious house, with hills behind and a flowing stream in front, ringed with ponds or pools, set about with bamboos and trees, a vegetable garden to the south, an orchard to the north...Then with two or three companions of philosophic bent discuss the Way or study some book... and so ramble through life at ease, with a cursory glance at Heaven and Earth and all that lies between, free from the censure of my fellowmen.

—T'ung Ch'ung-chang [A.D. 180-220][1]

Hundreds of millions of people are flocking to the national parks and wilderness areas every year. There is a logic to our urban discontent which defies assets, job security and air-conditioning. In this meditation, I examine the roots of urban uncertainty in myself and toy with the idea of moving to the country.

E very so often I receive a letter from the country. Sometimes the missive comes from a village in Alaska (I hate to call them "fishing villages" because that implies that the inhabitants do nothing but kill innocent creatures, yet the people I know up there are vegetarians). Or from a small town in Bhutan or Norway or New Mexico. It's all what I call country, a mythical realm of beginnings that has somehow avoided the day-to-day majority rule, though seldom its political and ecological hegemony.

Hegemony or not, the letters I have gotten indicate a rural sensibility very much alive and well in this world, even in small-town America, where the following words were written. I've edited a year's worth and changed the names so as to protect the uncitified.

Spring at last...I arrived a month before Henry and had some rough days, being so isolated on the land, no electricity (no light), mice taking over the cabin, and bad hay fever for three weeks. I finally managed to borrow a neighbor's old car to go and see a naturopath and acupuncturist for some relief. I love this quiet and simple lifestyle, I must say, yet some days I crave people contact and feel much better having found some balance.

Everything is transforming before my eyes, daily. Bulbs becoming miracles, soil giving way to plants I've never even seen. Must have been in the bird turd. There's a bug attacking the leaves of one of our elms and I don't know what to do about it. I've also seen a wolf. And know exactly what to do about him: wait. Naked. At night. You know how I feel about wolves. I must have been one, in another life. Don't mention I said that to Henry. He's older, more conservative, as you know. And I don't wonder that he's never warmed to my wolf fetish. Or my cougar fetish. But I can tell you, I'm awfully excited!

Summer... Henry arrived in mid-June with my folks, in a 1980 Datsun they gave us. Now the solar panel is hooked up for lights (Henry has read everything on the subject and seems bent on converting everyone to a soy-bean diet and solar power. So far he's batting a pretty good average in these woods (but, of course, up here, anything new sounds good.) The four foot high weeds he's cut with a gas weed trimmer. The mice are gone, by their own inclination—I don't know where to, down the road, I imagine—and so is my hay fever. We see deer, white little fannies, lots of nectar-crazed humming-birds, and last night watched an ermine tracking a small rabbit for five minutes in our driveway before pouncing at it. The rabbit, thank God, got away. Amazing sight.

There has been only one day of rain in weeks, and a record 100° temperature so I water the garden a lot. Bugs are eating everything, so it's a challenge organically. I've planted 90 tomatoes, 40 peppers, 30 squash, broc-

coli, corn and other seeds. We really need a caretaker here when we're gone to keep up with the weeds, pruning, etc.

Fall...The winds have started up. That time of year. Very little rain. Maybe the greenhouse effect. As far as our own greenhouse, the herbs are thriving. I mist them, after doing yoga every morning, and see the sun rise over the distant volcano. I'm doing massage therapy work, and volunteering a few hours a week with the call-in crisis center twenty miles away. There's more child and sexual abuse than alcoholism. You'd think, with all this gorgeous scenery around, that people would be more mellow. Reading Jane Austin. We're doing pretty good. Maybe just a little stir-crazy with the thought of our 11th winter up here soon upon us.

Winter...Henry's been out of it for weeks, having broken a wrist cross-country skiing up on the glacier. He misses his sculpture. The plight of the moose is heartbreaking this year. With so much snowfall, moose on the peninsula are dying of starvation at a rate of one per day. Two moose were just shot by the junior high school because the animals were too weak to stand. Supposedly, moose can become aggressive when people start feeding them, then demanding food from anyone, so we're supposed to stand back and watch them starve. I can't deal with that. And I have never seen any but the kindest moose. There are two moose sleeping in our backyard that look weak, but not starving yet. I've put out food, but it freezes up right away and the moose don't seem to notice it. I'm not sure what else to do. There are about three feet of snow at our house. I'm counting the days until Spring...

March... We figured it out—I should say, I figured it out. You probably know that I get hay fever. Well, would you believe it, that sonofagun has nothing to do with HAY! How do I know, well hay sits well atop snow. And one night I was sitting around reading through some of our art books and there was this series of paintings by Monet—hay, lots of hayricks—and then I got to thinking, horses eat hay, why not the moose?

You see one of the two had died on our property and we had to call in the county to take it away. The worst experience you can imagine. Not the smell, on account of how cold it was. But just the thought of a moose dying in our yard while we were snug inside. Nature can be horrible. That's when I had this brainstorm.

So Henry went into town, filled the Datsun with hay (it came from some other town, pre-packaged, incredibly expensive—whatever happened to the good old days?) and we started spreading it all over the place. Now we've got the entire regional moose population living with us. They love hay! I'm afraid to ask a vet if it's actually good for them. But now, there have been no deaths in our area, though hunters have started poking around. I've warned the bastards but I feel very anxious about the situation. As for the moose, they're eating us out of house and cabin. And, I'm not *sneezing. I'm counting the days until the snow melts and the grass thaws so that they can get down to serious business, as nature intended, and so can we...*

Whenever I hear from such friends, an inner dream of reason is tapped. It's as though I want to believe in the cozy universal prayer of rural places. I want to believe that despite there being millions of years of evolution between a flower and a human admirer, that the links are more crucial than the differences. Short of those links, we are non-existent. It's easy to hide behind information; to espouse the facile truth that god is in the details, a city principle. The rural strikes of links, the unknown, the unexplored, the past, the future, the soul, of reincarnation and exile, of poetry and birds, of monks and privacy and sublime truths that encompass god's details—every miracle known to the planet (dragonflies and Tiger Lilies, yarrow and Feverfew, Shasta daisies and Morning Glories)—but also the larger metaphors which these lovely creatures intimate in the human imagination.

When I think "rural," I am tossed and torn by the city which inhabits me. Hundreds of cities. Of the vast unchecked assemblage of toxins percolating into the drinking water of Milan, which I sampled a few years ago atop the largest garbage dump in Europe; or the total lack of safe drinking water, or of any kind of hygiene, in the dozens of Calcuttas of the world. That I dwell in a city, physically, part of the time, is far less important than the fact that cities are situated within my head most of the time.

Most consciousness is equivalent to urbanity. The city is an infuriating contradiction because we love and despise it, both; are trapped within its walls but see no real walls, nothing particularly stopping us from fleeing into the countryside, that mythical "first person rural," to borrow Noel Perrin's expression. Trapped because we cannot easily flee the idea of the city, even once we've made up our minds to do so.

There are wonderful aspects to every city, obviously. In his "Democratic Vistas," the same Walt Whitman who would pay homage to nature in one of the most sustained ecological rhapsodies ever written (*Leaves of Grass*) spoke of the "splendor," the "sane and heroic life" of a city like New York where he lived. In *Specimen Days* Whitman likened New York's hordes to some marvelous ocean tide. Nathaniel Hawthorne talked up "the wild life of the streets" and commented on their unforgettable charm. And on his lecture tours West, the great transcendentalist, Ralph Waldo Emerson, constantly praised "magnificent hotels" and wonderful streets. In a slightly different tilt, Jules de Goncourt, writing in his and his brother Edmund's *Journal* on July 1, 1856, tells us that "standing before the canvas of a good landscape painter, I feel myself more in the country than when I am in the middle of a field or wood."

The city's hold on our inner compass reading—what I called above its hegemony—is incalculably prolific. "Appreciation of wilderness began in the cities," wrote Roderick Nash, "the literary gentleman wielding a pen, not the pioneer with his axe." The great cities of the world have always been sources of wonder, magnets of psychological spoils, the place where human restlessness was always measured or applied. Cities like the legendary Kublai Khan's Cambaluc; or Cordoba under the reign of Abd-ar-Rahman III, in the mid-10th century, that great metropolitan think-tank of poets, philosophers and politicans. Or Persepolis, built in the late sixth century before Christ, the royal residence of the Achaemenid Kings; or Old Baghdad, capital of the Abbasid caliphs; and the other great spasms of culture and learning and desire—Alexandria, Aix-la-Chapelle, Aachen, Versailles, Titian's Venice, Reconstructionist Charleston, Pierre l'Enfant's original Washington D.C., fin-de-siècle Budapest and Vienna, St. Petersburg during the reign of Alexander III, Paris in the 1880's, Lucio Costa's Brasilia, the San Francisco of Herb Caen, the Boston of Bellamy.

Habitable metaphors, engineered in the cities, long ago began to invest the countryside. We know that human life began in the countryside and only much later proliferated to the extent of a city. But once that process was complete, a migratory reversal was set in motion. Roman poets were among the first to voice a nostalgia for the country and a disgust with the city. Domesticated wilderness had begun to fuel a commerce between isolation and congestion.

The city has a strange hold on consciousness. As the population creates and inhabits its cities, ideas create and inhabit their languages. If, as many have argued, we think with language, then this simultaneous colonizing of thought and of thought's words, condemns all metaphor to an urban point of reference. The past, which is biological, is thus subsumed in the syntactic present. As the possibilities for original terrestrial exploration diminish; even as the countryside fills up with people, the mind veers close upon Thoreau's dictum that there is no place we should look for wilderness but within ourselves, wherever we may be.

Similarly, following a partial ascent of Mount Ventoux, the poet Petrarch was rudely reminded of an oft-quoted passage from the *Confessions* in which St. Augustine had commented on mankind's capacity for seeking out the sea, the mountains, the desert, without ever casting his glance inward.

What then, is rural? A suburban ideal? That region of uncut forest on the far peripheries of urban chaos? A condition of human existence that is less stressful, less full of unessential busy work? The utopian theorists of the 19th century—Robert Owen, Fourier, Saint-Simon, Proudhon, among others—following Renaissance and classical Greek prototypes, like that described in Plato's *Republic*, with its total recommended population of 5000 individuals, prompted a mélange of American, egalitarian experiments. These rural communities were modeled upon the economy of nature. They sought to merge the city with the wilderness, whose likely byproduct was to be the noble savant, part gentleman farmer, part scholar, in the mode of Jefferson at Monticello and Hector St. John Crèvecoeur near Chester, New York, as described in his *Letters From an American Farmer*. The specific goals varied: social equality, feminism, communism, Marxist aesthetics, population control, free love, free libraries, free education, a general nature worship. For more than a century, such groups as the Shakers, George Rapp's Economy Community near Pittsburg, the German Mennonites, the Community of True Inspiration, founded near Buffalo in 1843, and John Noyes' Brook

Farm, attracted tens of thousands of disciples to a belief in the perfectibility of neighbors, of a nature rendered humane and comfortable.

At the same time, cemeteries became fashionable as park land. The Hudson River, Fontainbleau, Barbizon, Luminist, Intimist and Impressionist schools of painting seized upon these burial grounds, all garden space in general. They were transformed, in some cases, into the inner focus of whole cities, most notably in the designs by Frederic Law Olmsted for Central Park in New York.

By the early 20th century, the phrase "back to nature" was the rage. Jack London, Teddy Roosevelt and John Muir had celebrated the call of the wild, over one million automobiles had already bumped along the dirt roads into Yosemite National Park, as the last of the native Southern Miwok Indians were forced out of the Valley, and the Boy Scouts of America (founded in 1907) had become an instant success.

Then, one morning, on August 10, 1913, a middle-aged graphic artist by the name of Joseph Knowles stripped naked and plunged into the Maine woods with the idea of living off the land like Adam for 60 days. He made his own clothes from bark, lured a bear into a pit and killed it for his food, and basically proved to Americans that the wilderness could be conquered. When he re-emerged on October 4th of that year, he was welcomed as a homecoming hero. His subsequent book, *Alone in the Wilderness,* was to sell 300,000 copies.[2]

In 1933, at a time when one would have assumed that economic priorities would have come first, the wilderness ethic reached philosophical preeminence, not only in America, but in Scandinavia. It was in that year that both Aldo Leopold and Bob Marshall first published their ideas concerning the necessity of wilderness.[3] Leopold went on to integrate these first principles into his American classic, *Sand County Almanac.*

And it was also in 1933 that Thor Heyerdahl, age 19, then a zoology student at the University of Oslo, and his 20-year-old girlfriend Liv, convinced their families and professors to support an extended journey to Polynesia where the young (unmarried) scientists intended (officially) to study the fauna of a primitive setting. In actuality, their plan consisted simply of living off the land, bereft of manufactured food, medicines, clothing, weaponry, money, in short, of any semblance of civilization. They did so, more or less, for a year, and Heyerdahl's book *Fatu-Hiva - Back to Nature* (London, 1974) chronicles the mixed experience.

Pale and white from city living, Liv and Heyerdahl stepped off their caïque without the slightest idea of how to deal with an irate Roman Catholic missionary, mosquitoes, poisonous eels and centipedes, and often hostile islanders.

Nostalgia for music and the other fine arts, the need of medicine when Liv's foot became dangerously infected, and a certain curiosity to understand the migratory evolution of the Marquesan islanders, were all pressing vestiges of Heyerdahl and Liv's past; a civilized past which came quickly to cast a somber tone over their rustling moonlit nights. Science and survival commingled. All around them were the details of city mind begging to be analyzed and written up —microscopic plant plankton, the perpetual surf, shoals of fish, swarms of sea-birds, juicy mountain mangos, the ravages of elephantiasis on village populations, the manner of constructing a bamboo cabin, the method of capturing river shrimp and the discovery of ancient rock petroglyphs (*tikis*).

Soon the couple's hair had grown longer and their bodies brown, as the Marquesas revealed themselves to be a paradise of fruits and vegetables. Heyerdahl and Liv moved high onto a tropical upland slope where their days drifted by like so many thunder showers and sunsets. And, in the end, they crossed over the Touaouoho Mountains and settled with the last living cannibal on the island, along with his adopted daughter.

Heyerdahl writes: "A seemingly naked person came running towards us between the trees... Tei Tetua ran like a young mountain goat. He was weather-beaten and sun-tanned all over and wore nothing but a bag around his loins, tied to a waist-string of bark. The old man was muscular and agile as if he were half his real age. His whole face seemed to grin as he laughed with happy animation, showing teeth as perfect as those of the ancient skulls under our bed. When I gave him my hand and said 'kaoha,' he grabbed it laughing and writhing like a shy boy short of words. His whole person was almost bursting with restrained energy. He just did not seem able to express all he had to say after years of loneliness. 'Eat pig!' he finally exclaimed. 'When pig is finished we eat cock. When cock is finished we eat more pig!'

Then he bounded away like a young boy, down to his cluster of huts and began shouting at his bristly semi-wild boars."

Speaking with the cannibal about Marquesan "cultural history," Tei Tetua told them, "If someone died young it was because he fell from a palm tree, was caught by a shark, or was hit on the head by a war-club and eaten by an enemy.…'And what do you do with those you kill?'" he then asked. To which Heyerdahl replied that Westerners buried their dead. The cannibal was amazed, "truly disgusted at such barbaric waste." Heyerdahl relates that Tei Tetua then said, "Imagine killing people only to bury their flesh in the ground. Did nobody come and dig it up again when it was matured?" Reflecting on these matters, the Norwegian summarized by saying, "We are educated to run a bayonet into a living person, but not to run a fork into one who is already dead." It was just one of many dichotomies which came to haunt the city-bred scholar.

Heyerdahl and Liv learned how to play a nose-flute, that human flesh tastes like a sweet potato, something of the art of trepanation, of silence, and of how to deal with nothing to do. Eventually, their science, the city in them, had seemingly vanished. For months their serenity was unbroken, the coastal winds keeping mosquitoes away, until one day a horde of curious Marquesans and their children arrived from a village on the other side of the island and never left again, taking full advantage of Tei's abundant hospitality. There, on the remote wild mountains of Fatu-Hiva, the noise and commotion soon became too much for the young Westerners, who were reminded of downtown Oslo. They finally fled the scene, waited miserably for weeks in a cave, and ultimately caught a Tahitian schooner back to Europe.

Heyerdahl summed up his ambiguous experiences by stating, "Wild geese had no liver trouble; elephants and giraffes had healthy teeth and normal blood pressure. Physical disturbances increase with distance from natural conditions." But then this was only half of the truth. Liv was compelled to add, "One can't buy a ticket to paradise."

The relationship between the city and the country remains philosophically obscure, an inadvertence, nomads and fast food, olive groves and skyscrapers, time measured in seasons, or in exits; the quality of a harrow or of a microwave oven. If one adopts the existential engineering point of view, tools are tools, time is time, people are people. A Tibetan village or Greenwich Village. In nature, even the simplest coral reef yields a vision of extraordinary city-like complexity, with all the attendant symbiotic, mutualist, commensural and predatory relationships of Biology 101. A single leaf reveals in its veins a causeway of borders and stomatic cells, cubes, geographical fences, the so-called Fibonacci mathematical series pertaining to the growth of every organism, evident throughout nature, and all in a square inch, wherein the life force has ordered itself.

I don't think the mechanism of order has any more or less meaning than the mechanism of chaos. The disparities, the confusions that mark both cities and wilderness, will never, and probably should never, be resolved by human learning.

Order or chaos. The answer lies not in rural or urban, city or wilderness, but in the ecological self, whose world is yet to be discovered. To probe for even a moment inside ourselves is to be cast back to 1492 and before; to be confronted by the unknown.

Nevertheless, most of us need little coaxing, I'm sure, to appreciate the difference between city and country, even if we're not sure what to do about it. There is a lasting sobriety in the, by now, trite declaration, "in wildness is the preservation of the world." Wilderness is our only compass reading for getting our bearings inwardly, for seeing just how far we've journeyed away from ourselves. Never mind that the best compasses can be bought at Abercrombie & Fitch, or L. L. Bean, or at any number of mountain-climbing shops, in the city. The compasses I'm actually referring to are in the mind.

There's been much economic and technological debate in the last twenty years —as well as a few ethical questions raised—about our colonizing Mars. Why do I fear a future letter from the Martian countryside? With its description of invigorating cold, Himalayan-sized peaks, gorgeous calderas, ancient rivers, Arctic permafrosts and astounding views? And who knows, even a profusion of living lichens inside the surface rocks, as have been found, under similar conditions, in the Dry Valleys of Antarctica. A post-modernist paradise in which mankind will believe its own propaganda in asserting that we have finally transcended nature.

I truly do, I fear that day when the first letter reaches Earth via radio waves and an ingenious gallium arsenide chip, written from inside a computerized sealed dome, and in its closing lines I read the words, "But what has happened to us?"

[1]T'ung Ch'ung-chang [A.D.180-220] quoted in Arthur Waley, "Life Under the Han Dynasty: Notes on Chinese Civilization in the First and Second Centuries A.D.," *History Today*, 3, p. 94, 1953.
[2]See Roderick Nash's account of Knowles, in his book *Wilderness and the American Mind*, pp.141-142, third edition, Yale University Press, 1982.
[3]Leopold did so in his essay "The Conservation Ethic," *Journal of Forestry*, 31 (1933), 6324-43; and Marshall, in his contribution to *A National Plan for American Forestry*, 73rd Congress, 1st Session, Senate Document 12, 2 vols. (March 13, 1933) I, pp. 469-470.

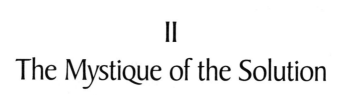

II

The Mystique of the Solution

Let us not run the world hastily...
Let us give prolonged attention to the future,
And let us give due regard to the consequence of things,
And that is an account of our last step.

—Yoruba liturgy[1]

We have grown up believing in solutions. Solutions to everything. The national debt, ants in the kitchen, headaches. But the world requires no solution. The world is perfect.

E. B. White once remarked that when he awoke each morning he didn't know whether to save or savor the world. That world can be safely divided between those who think everything's fine and those for whom the world is rotten. My wife is one who will not hear of problems; whose optimism is stubborn, though never blind. She knows precisely why she's happy and what it takes to get there. My grandmothers, conversely, were both vigorously entrenched in the opposite camp; always dusting, forever complaining about the Capitalists (both ladies were disenfranchised souls from the Old Country), admonishing the butcher, gesturing with disgust at the nightly television news.

Every day, in every household, someone like my wife discerns a miracle while a wise old grandma seizes upon a catastrophe. And while my mate rejects excessive belaboring of the negative, closing off her mind to those who delight in detailing disaster, she is never remiss about her own rage. There is a cauldron seething in her; a fanatical Joan of Arc who would right all wrong and give herself to every stray sparrow. She is, in other words, a gentle, angry, compassionate, Earth-loving woman whose priorities are not easily sustained in a world that basically ignores good people. Like my grandmothers, she is basically alone, fending for herself. Unlike my grandmothers, she knows it, and her life is one valiant effort to be joyous and caring in spite of the adversity we must all grapple with. I admire that.

Both personalities—that of my spouse, and of my grandmothers—are taken with the idea of solutions; of a life that is constantly subject to being solved. Only the methods vary. I don't know where they all came by this habit and what convinced them that solutions were needed in the first place. Grandmothers and spouses alike marshall impressive evidence and impeccable logic in support of their views, and the world does not hold back its confirmation, in either case.

For my taste, the Rabbinical sensibility purports to a compelling middle ground.

Consider the great 19th century Rabbi of Warsaw as he lay upon his deathbed, surrounded by thousands of disciples. The chief initiate whispered in his ear, "Oh wise and beloved one, what is your final revelation?" To which the dying holy man, after long moments of contemplation, uttered weakly, "Life is a river!"

In astonished whispers, the Rabbi's wisdom reverberated as an echo between lips; like a tidal wave of epiphany and incantation; like the wind through winter wheat on the great steppes of the Ukraine, where—during blizzards—people frequently get lost and die somewhere between the kitchen door and the outhouse in the backyard; until the last disciple in the far reaches of the temple, poking his head just inside the great corridor which led to the Rabbi's chamber, heard the news.

"Life is a river?" he muttered in perplexity, scratching his beard, blinking with a tick of unrecognition. "But what does it mean?"

Others nearby were stunned by this young yeshiva bucher's audacity, this nobody; this iccch nothing person. "What does it mean?" they repeated, annoyed but unnerved. Until, like a tidal wave in reverse, the perplexity gained momentum, from disciple to disciple—"But what does it mean?" went the horrified or embarrassed refrain; like all things in nature which come home to rest; like karma, like exhausted whales and penguins, even like children who grow old. Until the unnatural avalanche of queries, born upon a thousand sets of bewildered lips, reached the ears of the chief disciple.

Not happy about this awkward task, he waited until he could wait no longer. "But what does it mean, oh Great One?" the disciple inquired, his humility betraying philosophical agitation.

The Great Rabbi looked up at the ceiling, considered all things and, with a whimsy appropriate to his station, replied, "Alright, so maybe life's not a river!"

We are raised to solve problems. At the age of two, I contemplated my crib in an effort to plot my intricate escape. At three, I was focused on reaching cookie jars by means of stepladders and chairs in the kitchen. By four, I was fixated on eluding the doctor's annual innoculations. At five, I was troubled by the fingering of some Mozart sonatina. At six, there were bullies in school. At seven, the teacher was the problem, and no solution was in sight. My eighth birthday brought the solution, a new teacher who was beautiful. And that's when my problems really began. For the next eight years, that dilemma only escalated, from nerves to hormones to fantasy life, exacerbated by magazines at the local drugstore. My earliest algebra problems were no match for girl problems. But one night, at the tender age of sixteen, the solution was finally discovered, and it was spectacular, though I won't repeat her name.

By then it was clear to me that Americans could solve any problem, or so it was assumed: the availability of credit, a lighter automobile engine, space stations, the water level, bigger tomatoes, inflation, declining literacy, the problem of minorities, the poor, the dispossessed.

However, Vietnam was a big problem. And what solutions were offered blew up in our collective face. The killing of the Kennedys, of Martin Luther King, of the students at Kent State, added to my suspicion that Americans, like everybody else, were vulnerable. We didn't have all the answers; we didn't even have the right questions.

Problems and solutions had shaped my growing up. And then one day I realized that there were no problems and solutions in this world, only people with problems and people in need of solutions. The world was perfect.

Twenty years after the pull-out from Vietnam, Americans seem more divided than ever before on this business of solutions. As I write this essay (July, 1992), a better than average spate of new solutions and new problems for life on planet Earth are being propagated all around me.

Here are a few of the new solutions being promoted just now:

There is increasing momentum for Jeremy Rifkin's "beyond beef" campaign, an inspired effort to cut beef consumption in half in the next ten years, and to break the back of the international beef cartel. That will help solve rampant animal abuse problems, water problems, hunger problems, agricultural problems.

A new bill introduced by Rep. Gerry Studds, a Massachusetts democrat, promises to encourage lawmakers to expand the premise under which the Endangered Species Act was codified twenty years ago; to implement far-reaching plans to protect not just the species, one by one, but whole habitats. This is basic ecology, but the law is only now beginning to catch on. At present, something like 650 plants and animals in the United States are officially endangered under that law. But thousands of species are actually at risk because their entire ecosystems are being systematically demolished.

In court, the National Resources Defense Council has won its suit against the EPA, thus forcing the agency to prevent four more carcinogenic pesticides from entering the human food chain. That leaves over fifty legal carcinogenic pesticides in domestic use. Plenty of room for more solutions.

And then there is all that Bill Clinton/Al Gore news: their electrifying energy at the Democratic Convention; their graceful, smiling solutions to the abortion dilemma, AIDS, the deficit, gay rights, the trade imbalance, the capital gains tax issue, the fuel efficiency issue, the nuclear power problem, the crisis in education and child support, family values and crime, a host of foreign policy problems, labor policy and job training issues, the Medicare crisis, the welfare crisis, the global warming crisis, the Eastern European, the PRC, the Japanese, the South African and the Iraqi crises.

And there's all that Bush news: the House approving a $252-billion dollar defense bill; the Bush-Yeltsin announcement to end the "Nuclear Nightmare" by slashing stockpiles in half by the year 2003. Of course, that will leave nearly 7000 nuclear weapons between them, each one of which is vastly more powerful than that which annihilated Hiroshima and Nagasaki. The elation attendant on this historic accord lasted for about a day. Within the week, U.S. voters were prepared, by all accounts, to elect a virtual stranger to the office of President, because they wanted a change. Apparently, historic accords are not enough. Along comes a billionaire with a phlegmatic temper who boasted, "OK—I'M YOUR CHANGE!" as if from a Bavarian beerhall, and that was enough to inspire the confidence of Americans who would be willing to turn over 3500 nuclear weapons to a spoiled, evasive cattleman, a condition of mass gullibility and ignorance reminiscent of Germany in the 1920's and 30's.

Meanwhile, in the Commonwealth of Independent States, several warheads were missing, and several of the nations with their fingers on the nuclear panic buttons were battling each other: Azerbaijanis in Nakhichevan, Ossetians in northern Georgia, ethnic Russians and Ukrainians in Moldova, and Armenians in Nagorno-Karabakh. It seemed that rather than forging greater security, the Bush/Yeltsin agreement had merely benumbed the public's justifiable uneasiness. More problems, more partial solutions.

And while Bush was making strides to ease nuclear fears at home, his administration was also preparing to wipe out the northern spotted owl—a typical contradiction—in order to sustain a few trivial and malicious jobs. This is particularly disturbing in light of the fact that, according to the Sierra Club, more than 90 percent of the ancient forests of Washington, Oregon and California have been destroyed by the timber industry, in collaboration with various sectors of the U.S. government. George Bush appointed six of the seven members of an Endangered Species Committee which has the unprecedented ability to override the Endangered Species Act, if it sees fit (a power which the committee exercised under Jimmy Carter when it resolved to kiss an endangered fish species, the Snail Darter, good-bye). Now, once again, by a vote of 5 to 2, the committee has decided to allow the Bureau of Land Management to sell off thirteen additional old-growth forest areas in the Northwest to logging interests. The sale will mean big profits for a few CEOs; big profits for foreign companies that receive the whole logs before milling them, finishing them, and shipping them back to the U.S. as furniture; and it will mean jobs for a few thousand people who would be much more mercifully served by a pink slip that induced them to go out and get re-trained in a professional work arena that is not doomed, sooner or later, to obsolescence. And one that did not kill harmless owls and bears and countless other species, not to mention 2000 year old trees that never did anything to anybody. Problems and non-solutions.

And meanwhile, Saddam Hussein was mocking the U.N. inspectors and Clinton and Gore were ascending rapidly in the polls.

That was July, 1992. In many respects, it reminded me of July, 1972, and July, 1962.

It even called to mind an image of the 15th century, at what is today Bandelier National Monument, near Los Alamos.

In that eternal Canyon of Frijoles, of beans, the south-facing cliff dwellings, with their once inhabited remnants, stairways to the stars, bat caves, kivas, petroglyphs and sacred pedestals, look out over a lush valley twenty miles long, a half-mile wide. Bear and mountain lion and a variety of snakes and squirrels and deer still inhabit this paradise. Tourists like myself scramble over the creek-winding trail, climb up the fixed ladders over rock, look out into dreamtime, where New Mexico's clouds and lightning display their false machismo for a few minutes, before passing down the rim.

We, too, move on, at some instant of restlessness or resignation; climbing back down the ladders in order to return to the world of problems and solutions which begins up on the rim above Bandelier, where mile after mile of barbed wire closes off the sinister enclave of Los Alamos, and signs discourage would-be trespassers with warnings of "High Explosives." Explosives which, just fifty years ago, were deemed the solution to the Soviet threat.

But the Native Americans who once called this valley home half-a-millenium ago had no high explosives, no restlessness and resignation, no problems and no solutions. Or that is the romantic temptation: to believe in a past whose greatest gift, the freedom its inhabitants most probably relished, was its freedom from solutions. Of course, with hindsight, one knows that the innocent inhabitants of Bandelier (named after the Swiss anthropologist) were sitting ducks in the path of the white homesteaders.

I call it a realm of mystique because places like Bandelier and works of art like Bach's "St. Matthew's Passion," Purcell's "Fantasies" for strings, Shakespeare's *A Midsummer Night's Dream,* or the whole body of New Mexico, as seen and painted by American master Victor Higgins, and others, intimate that freedom.

My grandmothers died unhappy, I believe; caught up in the world's turmoil; in the minor daily troubles of Squirrel Hill (Pittsburgh) and of East Denver; while my wife and her mother and my own parents live life determined to enjoy it, not unaware of the turmoil, but neither too obsessed with it.

Somewhere between our complaining, our lawsuits, our wringing of hands and our miracle cures, there is a personal Bandelier, an artform, a middleground that holds the key to a fulfilling life. Dickens called it when he reminded us that every era is the worst and the best of times. Of course he was also dissecting the human being who is the engineer of those times; whose inner psyche determines all. To be honest, the world is the world. It is as it should be. And nothing you or I say, or do, is likely to alter that fact. Which means that whatever problems and solutions confront us, with all their contradictions, false promises, paradoxical impacts, and fragmentary panoramas, are of our own making and have little or nothing to do with the greater planetary reality, that biological stream of sentience which awaits us the moment we are willing to admit it to ourselves. Saul Bellow once wrote that personality is destiny. And that about sums it up, I suspect.

[1]Yoruba liturgy, in The Beginnings of Early Man and His Gods, by H. R. Hays, p. 346, G. P. Putnam's Sons, New York, NY, 1963.

III
The Search for Paradise

By virtue of offering to you, assembly of Buddhas
Visualized before me, this mandala built on a base,
Resplendent with flowers, sprinkled with perfumed water,
Adorned with Mount Meru and the four continents,
As well as the sun and moon. May all sentient beings share in
its good effects.

—Geshe Namgyal Wangchen[1]

Figures compiled by the IRS indicate that donations to churches [not
counting income from stock dividends and bond yields, or profits from their
businesses] are nine billion dollars a year in those collection plates. That
works out to over 173 million every Sunday. This does not include anything
willed to them, either. That's a pretty costly seat in heaven you all are
praying for.

—Madalyn Murray O'Hair, *American Atheist*[2]

The one principle animating every organism is the will to survive. Not surprisingly, the psyche has its own physical requirements, which collectively might be called paradise. This meditation seeks to discover that paradise in the one place we are likely to always find it, nature. Nature all around us. Nature inside us.

Take a few moments and visualize your own paradise...

What is it?

Some will discover that the word itself is inadequate to convey the range of possibilities, fragments and irresolutions that come to mind. We sample images from what we know, have seen, have heard. The images come together in a mosaic, a wish-list, whose cohesiveness is in ourselves, but not necessarily in the world, or not all in one piece, one place, or at one time. As an old Turkish saying goes, "It was some time, and it wasn't any time, when the flea was a barber and the camel a street-crier, and I was rocking my grandfather's cradle."

Is paradise merely a form of pathos, another noble savage, an anachronism, a distant view? Or is it a living feeling? A romance? Something I can touch, this paradise? And from whence has the word, the urging, arisen? The ancient Persian word, *faradis*, referred to an enclosed hunting preserve for the exclusive pleasure of royal families. In early Mesopotamia, *Dilmun* was the land of the immortals, a place to which King Gilgamesh aspired. In the *Gilgamesh* epic, at least one human being had reached that place, Utnapishtim. Was he happy? Presumably.

In ancient Greece, *Arcadia* referred to a specific mountain region in the center of the country that enjoyed a temperate climate and gave rise to large and healthy montagnards. In reality, according to Aristotle's student, Dicaearchus, Arcadia was like any other place, perhaps even too crowded. Indeed, Arcadia's seat of political power was located in a town called Megalopolis, not the most auspicious sounding Garden of Eden. Dicaearchus looked back in time to some earlier era of tranquility and bliss.

Nevertheless, European history came to idealize Arcadia, a place in the mind which continues to symbolize a pastoral vision encompassing a life style and an aesthetic given to leisurely contemplation, the creation of art, the meandering of sheep and the odd white marble temple on a remote hill.

I know of no better iconographic portrayals of this passion, this composite setting than that of Nicolas Poussin's "St. John on Patmos," (Art Institute of Chicago), Giorgione's "Tempesta," and "Fête Champêtre," (in the Venice Accademia, and the Louvre), or Jean-Baptiste Corot's many depictions of the Villa D'Avray outside of Paris.

In all of these paintings, the artists have catapulted recognizable life into the world we should otherwise demand; the world most demonstrably of our own urgings and truth; the world we know, but have only been able to enjoy mentally.

Such dreamy pageants celebrate mauve and umber, early retirement, mollify most ordinary despair or gravity by capturing for an instant the permanence of an ideal.

But the ironies cascade. If one celebrates the flock, one also recognizes that, for example, during the English Renaissance, when Thomas More was obliquely rhapsodizing Norway in his work, *Utopia*, the sheep of England were massively dispossessing the peasant. The English wool industry impoverished the English farmer. Elizabeth I was compelled to enact legislation in 1601 forcing landowners to pay for the maintenance of the poor as a result of the sheep devastation.

If one hails the remnants of distant ages, the requisite marmoreal columns that so figure in the paintings of Poussin and Claude Lorrain, one must also acknowledge that these mighty parthenons were not just beautiful, but wreaked havoc with mountainsides, where the stone was quarried by slaves. In China, where once was wilderness, engineers erected their homage to nature and cosmology in massive assemblages of stone and wood, tearing down forests, mobilizing enormous labor forces, and creating cities—Ch'ang-an, the capital of the T'ang Dynasty, and Hang-chou, capital of the southern Sung—that would soon swell in the Middle Ages to over a million inhabitants.

Ch'ang-an was meant to be a paradise on earth, and to that end the earliest avenues were laid out. Indigenous trees were uprooted and replanted in straight lines. Twenty-two miles of wall were constructed in order to receive twenty-two miles of moonlight. Like the Forbidden City in Peking, every aspect of the construction symbolized the heavens, or the principles of the yin and the yang, despite the earlier cautions of China's premier philosophers, Lao-tzu, Chuang-tzu and Mencius, who had warned against tampering with nature. The Taoist notion of *feng-shui* pertains to humanity's ability to foster harmony, to adapt the residences of the living and the dead to nature. This ancient philosophical penchant in Chinese thought runs counter to the other, technological predilection that saw the development, within China, of piped natural gas, of paper manufacture and collar harnesses, and of huge cities.

But the ironies are even more complicated. For instance, even before the T'ang Dynasty, with its profusion of nature societies and ecological revelations, the harmonious, written word was causing widespread destruction in the form of calligraphic ink, a byproduct of soot, which in turn came from burnt pine, a literary rage which reduced whole mountains to carbon.

Of course, tampering is not tampering when it is religiously ordained, as it was in the Bible. Even China's legendary founder of the Hsia Dynasty, Yu, was said to have "opened up the rivers of the Nine Provinces and fixed the outlets of the nine marshes."

When Western explorers heard about the Kublai's summer retreat at Xanadu (Shang-tu), and when the Buddha's biographical details were Christianized into popular parable, another set of ecological paradoxes were soon to evolve. Asiatic slaves—exotic looking, the genetic wild strains of paradise—were imported to Italy. During the height of Neo-Platonist times, there were an estimated 400 Asian slaves held captive in Florence.

The quest for the Garden of Eden which fueled so much of European expansion, grew up in the lonely fields of the painter's brush and poet's brevity; on cave walls in Sinkiang Province, near modern Urumqi; or north-west of Kabul at Bamiya; at Kuca, in western Sinkiang, and at Tun-huang, where the monk Lo Tsun had seen a vision of 1000 Buddhas. Within a few centuries, European mapmakers like Paolo de Pozzo Toscanelli were point-ing out that the east coast of Asia —where these Biblical Gardens of Eden were most likely to be found—could be reached by sailing across the Atlan-tic. The Genoan, Columbus, was one of many adventurers who believed the rumor. All of Europe's monarchies harbored vast mercantilist expectations of the East, as they would the South, where it was said that "gold is obtained in great plenty, huge elephants abound, with wild trees of all sorts, and ebony; and the men are taller, handsomer, and longer lived than anywhere else." That was the historian Herodotus predicting the wave of discovery, 1500 years before.

All of which, as we know, led to the conquest of much of the world; to the annihilation of countless millions of tribal indigenes, and to the unchecked growth of money-driven economies, with its industrial mayhem and eco-logical angst.

And, as the conquistadores laid waste to the tropics, tropical natives were fleeing for their own dreamed-of lands to the West; to safe, gleaming El Dorados they had long mythologized.

The awareness of a psychologically traumatic era certainly pre-dates the modern age of environmental existentialism. Hieronymus Bosch, for example, graphically depicted the horrors that beset most of Europe throughout the 16th century. A century before that, the various illuminated *Book of Hours* manuscripts often portrayed the devastations wrought by pestilence and marauders.

For as long as we have any kind of documentation—nearly 60,000 years—there is evidence that virtually every society was fraught with self-doubt and a crisis of human nature. Ancient Greek and Roman, early Mayan, Khmer, Teotihuacan, Anasazi, and dozens of other cultures have vanished as a result of their ecological imbalance, which was represented in the art, and could be read, obviously, in the collective psyche.

To fix nature, as the Emperor Yu apparently tried, corresponds with the engineering mentality inherent to all civilizations—from the construction of Roman aquaducts, and Medieval marsh reclamation in the Low Countries, to bituminous coal smelting, steam power, the emergence of barbed wire, the Michigan Canal, the Holborn Viaduct-Pearl Street Station in New York (the first commercial venture using electricity), to Lloyd's of London, and the great financial empires of the 20th century.

Some time ago, I visited a Shinto mountain temple about twenty miles from Kyoto, where Thomas Edison is worshipped as a sort of deity. It was here that the inventor chose a bamboo filament from the forest to use in his first light bulb. He considered it the most perfect in the world. And it probably was. Shinto illumination. Enlightenment. A global revolution in energy, beginning in a silent, mystical bamboo glen. With such swings of the human pendulum, there is absolutely no predicting how powerful one's inner contemplation is likely to be.

And yet, reflecting upon the causes and consequences of civilization, the billions of personal dreams and delectations, the innocent child at play in the insane village world of a Bruegel, one is ever reminded of that frail word, "paradise." Of the somber irreconcilability which persists between person and species, mind and matter. We know, more or less, how we got here. How this slew of defects and of deleterious behavior, of grand endeavors and bland anonymities, invokes a readable history. There are criminals and madmen, quiet felicities and altruisms that layer our vestigial psyche. Throughout it all is the private moment which, inexhaustibly in thought, imagines action; tireless in action, seeks inwardly for meaning. And the nature of these tandem migrations is Nature herself.

That means (to me) that every thought is conditioned by its store of images and experience, nature reproducing in biology as in mind, but that we are free (in the sense of free will) to imagine as our whims and genes and personalities dictate. Giorgione and Claude Lorrain, Poussin and Corot were conditioned by historical circumstances that differed little from our own. They were engulfed in wars, physical assaults, madding crowds, and the general erosion of the commonwealth, even as the empires prided themselves on increasing technological sophistication. Ethical peril, insoluble social conundrums and the nostalgia for a Golden Age are part of an equation, it seems, which figures in any calculation, in any era, of personal survival.

In Giorgione's day (the late 15th, early 16th century), Venetian supremacy was challenged by the Vatican, by the Ottomans, by most leaders in Europe. Leonardo Da Vinci invented his submarine in an effort to help the Venetian Doge cope with the overwhelmingly bad military odds against him. Nevertheless, in a time of unprecedented inflation and political disarray, the young Giorgione found a way to reinvigorate that primeval vision of the imagination which has always sought psychic survival in the natural world.[3] There is an obvious corollary that is especially applicable to the end of this millennium. As the human collective becomes ever more entropic, the individual evolves more rapidly, necessarily takes on more psychological responsibility, and thus has the possibility of becoming more whole.

Marine biologists know that evolution occurs more rapidly in harsh places and at bad times. The Arctic and Antarctic, for example, are unique genetic breeding grounds, abundantly fertile, despite the bitter, desert-like conditions.

Similarly, economic, ideological and military hardships will inevitably result, sooner or later, in a dialetical, positive synthesis, documented by clinicians in dozens of fields, from Hegel, Schopenhauer and Spengler, to Marx, Freud and historian Arnold Toynbee. The one impulse throughout this process of breakdown and reaffirmation that recurs with the most dramatic flourish, is the idea of paradise, a word that has become synonymous with Nature.

If times of trouble characteristically inspire great art, if that pent-up promise and imagery of any culture reaches its zenith, or reflection, on the brink of destruction, then what I am suggesting is that certain individuals rise to the occasion. Dickens' London, his Coketown, was rife with "melancholy madness…people equally like one another, who all went in and out at the same hours…" There were rivers of ill-smelling dye and vast rattling buildings. It was this devastating and demented landscape that prompted his glorious novels, *Hard Times, Little Dorrit* and *Bleak House*. Wordsworth similarly saw the earliest trains spewing pollution through the Lake District and editorialized about the coming destruction of British nature, but did so while rendering compositions of sublime beauty, like "Tintern Abbey."

"Where is a people that does not plunder the wealth of another?" wrote the ancient poet of Qumran.[4] As the ecological avalanche comes closer, impinging with the full fury of its international, economic, social and political malaise, the individual psyche retreats, typically, for biological and ethical reasons, towards its own inner garden. Where are inner peace and purity consistent with outer prosperity? How can an individual inhabit that safe haven?

There are plenty of embraces, of course: voters canvassing others to register; activists shouldering regional and global burdens; people fighting specific battles in every conceivable domain. Volunteers with the homeless, the old and infirm, people helping people. There are British entrepreneurs working out alternative agricultural solutions in the mountains of the Cameroon, and conservation biologists in every country of the world seeking to preserve and stabilize animal and plant populations. Children and parents and loved ones are helping each other. Every individual gesture of compassion and beauty and joy combats the odd ineluctability of our neurosis and disgrace as a species. Such that, before long, whole neighborhoods seem destined, like the angels of a Fra Angelico fresco, to ascend to radiant heaven. There was this poignant sense of reversal in the hands-across-South Central, a peaceful show of community revival in the wake of the Los Angeles riots in April, 1992, as in the community efforts following Hurricane Andrew, or in the work of the U.N. peacekeeping forces.

Negative energy flow is easily transmuted into positive; Hell becomes Paradise, if not in such black and white terms, then by the simple commission of a good deed. As children, we helped older people across the street. Forty feet of archetypal commiseration, ingrained forever on the way to school.

I remember the day (I must have been eight years old) that my class was asked to draw the synagogue across the street from our public school. The other children produced myriad architectural semblances. I drew Auschwitz, or something like what I imagined the Nazi persecution of Jews to be all about. There were evil people parachuting out of the skies with wild machine guns pointing every which way and bullets flying and little girls screaming and mothers pulling out their hair. The crayon colors were vivid— I remember purple blood and orange hair and yellow screams and black Nazi helmets. The teacher was disturbed by my rendition and took me to see the principal and a school counselor. My mother, a painter herself, was very proud of me and told the school authorities that I was clearly making a statement, and cathartically clearing out the demons in my head.

What I was doing, I suppose, was working through a concern that could have only affected me distantly. I lost a good many relatives because of those Nazis, including my great grandmother, who was shot in the back and dumped into a mass grave. Many years later, the same child wandered across the grassy surface of Babiyar, on the fringe of Kiev, where some 60,000 Jews were tossed during World War II. I grew faint and began to weep inside as I stepped across the fresh sward which smelled so wonderful, while below were tens of thousands of agitating dead souls.

And then, one morning, I woke up and read about Nazi-style Serbian genocide of the Bosnians, and began to write this essay, surrounded by half-a-dozen palm trees and tropical liana, a Chinese elm and a blooming, prolix garden—Penstemon gloxinioides, Forget-Me-Nots, Anisodontea and Lisianthus — compliments of my mate.

Alone in the garden, surrounded by the week's newspapers, beneath the sky, I attempt to fashion a response which can truly address my feelings, put them into words—not just for the benefit of a readership, but for myself; to coin the pages that reflect my Self, in a slow process which begins with sudden, or evolving awareness, details and analysis, and continues to conviction. It happens seated, or reclining, in the mind, in the open air, looking out a window, pacing itself in spurts, waking up, going to sleep, on the written page. To communicate with others? To talk to myself? To know something more deeply?

How does the knowing, the page after page, get me closer to the paradise which yearns to be discovered in me? Is it, as Jean-Paul Sartre more than once remarked, a useless passion?

The early 20th century Alexandrian poet, Cavafy, speaks of Ithica—the old, run-down, port city of prehistory that so enticed great wanderers to its bountiful harbor and alluring bazaars. It was not Ithica, the city, but Ithica—the ideal—that reaches to mythology. All aesthetic and spiritual idealism atones, in its way, for reality, diverting attention, if it can, from the mundane.

Meditation is no different. In championing the Self, engendering an inner space that is inviolate and aware, that can, if so determined, lose its Self in selflessness, one has achieved Nature's probable ideal, which is Being.

Philosophers have debated Being and Becoming, particularly the Germans and Austrians, like Heidegger and Wittgenstein, and the Greeks, like Parmenides and Heraclitus, for a long time. This not surprisingly insatiable demand for Being is, like everything else in the world, conditioned by time, which means that Being must become something. Thought must become something. The accumulation of Being, or of thought, is tantamount to a new thing. We are always changing.

How is it, then, that in spite of all this ceaseless change, what the pan-Asiatic knows as *samsara*, paradise ever remains the same? Even in the inflated Self, after however many millennia of physics and economics and narcissism, the craving for its borders resembles no other wanderlust; the inner turmoil knows no other resolve; and regardless of our ecstasy or agony today, there is no better wild surmise tomorrow than that which we term, paradise.

As a psychology unto itself, complete with historical and aesthetic trappings, illustrations, and treasure maps, this paradise must be reckoned as the goal of all introspection. We may call it the desire for knowledge, or inner tranquility, universal peace or non-violence; an end to hunger, to meat-eating, to cruelty and ignorance; an apotheosis of every positive charge in the human pysche…However one designates this perennial garden in the grey matter, its reality can no longer be contested.

That means that dreamers are not merely dreamers; that idealists are the most rudimentary of people. There is, in the bold corners of the psyche, a storm-tossed sea, a directionless vessel, a captain bravely peering past the known, his faith lodged in the beyond. And what is it, this edge of the universe about which there has been so much theological and scientific speculation? I often wonder, having myself traversed quite a few of those hills beyond the horizon, which Kipling so entrancingly hailed. And which the late writer, Paul Zweig, likened to the very origins of what was ever worth talking about in the first place, namely, adventure.

We were all nomads. Our brains continue to be, even if some of us are now a little more content to remain seated in an even plot of able turf, somewhere.

In the unadulterated interstices of any given day, where the mind seeks momentary refuge in this paradise past, there is strength and survival; the knowledge that a kingdom exists, no matter how deep the avalanche all around us.

In the Rockies, there are wild roses which bloom under many feet of snow. By the time that icy vault has melted in the late spring, admitting for the first time a beam of sunlight, the rose is already a veteran. Nothing stops it. Nothing will. It has spent the whole dark winter wrestling with its potential, at peace within itself, just as the human soul has wrestled and waited millions of ancestral years in order to flourish for its time.

The paradise of which we all speak is biological. It has become psychological in as much as *Homo sapiens* partakes, like every other creature, of a bounty that is heartbreakingly generous.

There is nowhere necessarily to go with this. Though, elliptically, there is everywhere to be. All remedy and analysis; all comfort and love. Practical solutions, like a light bulb; grand expeditions, as those to Ithica—that cultivate the perfect sea breeze of a simile, the Medieval mystic's definition of a circle whose circumference is nowhere and whose center is everywhere.

In this psyche of paradise, the fashion of our survival lies waiting.

We may not have the tools or the wisdom or the circumstances to restore the wilderness to its "original" condition, but we can make sensitive choices that stem from the heart, the ancient psyche, and carry the authority of natural selection, of evolution whose purpose, apparently, is a rich palette, biodiversity. There is a fitting ideal, akin to what I have been describing as paradise, in that changing wilderness. As physiologist Jared Diamond discusses in a recent essay entitled "Must We Shoot Deer to Save Nature?"[5] the changes all around us require a dynamic response that is rooted to no one stubborn philosophy. For example, the "laissez-faire philosophy of reserve management," that do-nothing-nature-knows-best method of handling the world, may result in catastrophic attrition for those creatures whose primary predators have been wiped out by man. Diamond argues that—having destroyed the wolf and the grizzly bear, the tiger and the cougar—we must now prevent the deer from overpopulating and destroying their habitats, as they have been doing in at least one region in Missouri, the Fontenelle Forest. That because we have checker-boarded nature with our fences and highways and ranches and cities—forget right and wrong, it's done—that we are foolish to expect fragmented ecosystems to nurture healthy animal and plant hierarchies, as in the past. We must complete the cycle, says Diamond. We owe it to the world. I would suggest relocating them.

Giorgione and Corot came to terms with the lurking high density of Venice and Paris, which they described in the sunlit peripheries of their naturalistic visions. There was sound integration which actually lent to their art a most remarkable and truthful sense of inhabited wilderness.

Paradise, whose contours and texture and ecosystems are ever changing, remains a psychological need of all ages; it enters not so esoterically into our lives. We recognize that everything we do, say, hope for, hinges upon it. To speak of the environment is to speak of this primordial destiny. Of earth, of art, of all ideals, the mind's own sanctity, this place of the soil and the spirit. Being to Becoming. Ecology to Psychology.

[1] Geshe Namgyal Wangchen's *Awakening the Mind of Enlightenment—Meditations on the Buddhist Path*, Wisdom Publishers, London 1987.

[2] Madalyn Murray O'Hair, "*American Atheist*," Program 16, Sept.16, 1968, KTBC Radio-Austin, Texas, printed in O'Hair's *What On Earth Is An Atheist*, Arno Press and The New York Times, 1972.

[3] See the author's chapter on Giorgione in *A Vision Of Nature—Traces Of The Original World*, Kent State University Press, 1994.

[4] "Book of Mysteries," *Dead Sea Scrolls*, p. 398 in *More Light on the Dead Sea Scrolls—New Scrolls and New Interpretations, with Translations of Important Recent Discoveries*, by Millar Burrows, Viking Press, New York, 1958.

[5] pp. 2-8, *Natural History Magazine*, August 1992.

IV
The Soul of Jainism

He who looketh on creatures, big and small, of the earth, as his own self, comprehendeth this immense universe.

—from the teachings of the Jinas[1]

Jainism, one of the oldest religions in the world, has formulated an exquisite approach to solving all human dilemmas through inner non-violence. By detailing the carnage of both our thoughts and footsteps, Jain meditation has discovered the principle of minimizing violence at every moment, every day; a principle that is not difficult to live by once it has been deeply thought out.

I encountered my first glimpse of Jainism in a white marble, spotlessly clean temple many years ago, whilst travelling through western India. It was late in the day. Birds were flocking overhead, where a large sculptured spire rose from the center of the temple towards a magenta twilight. Upon approaching the entrance, a white-robed gentleman quietly surveyed my person, then requested that I be so kind as to leave my watch outside the temple. He explained that leather—the watchband—was not permitted inside the sacred space of Jainism. He used the "ism" rather than referring to the temple itself, and this complicated contraction of the language set me to wondering.

Not long after that, I realized I was a Jain at heart.

There are some 10,000,000 Jains today, mostly in India, perhaps 30,000 in the United States. And they are to be found in many other countries, from Ethiopia to Canada. Until the last century their religion was frequently confused by Western scholars with both Hinduism and Buddhism. But, in fact, it is arguably the oldest living faith in the world, dating back tens of thousands of years. There are incontrovertible Jain documents as early as the 10th century B.C., 600 years prior to the emergence of Buddhism. Unlike the later Brahmanic spiritualist traditions in Central Asia, with their bouquets and contagia of deities, the Jains worship no god. Worship, according to them, is a form of interference, and interference is counter to nature. They revere nature. That is their essential characteristic. The semantics are obtuse. What is the difference between "revere" and "worship" one asks? Perhaps the important distinction rests upon the idea of God, which the Jains dismiss as anthropomorphic, whereas Nature —the word, the concept, the surreality—necessarily transcends any focal point of conceptualization.

By analogy, Immanuel Kant's struggle with pure reason bears striking similarity to the concept of nature in Jainism. Kant writes: "Our reason (*Vernunft*) has this peculiar fate that, with reference to one class of its knowledge, it is always troubled with questions which cannot be ignored, because they spring from the very nature of reason, and which cannot be answered, because they transcend the powers of human reason...reason becomes involved in darkness and contradictions, from which, no doubt, it may conclude that errors must be lurking somewhere, but without being able to discover them, because the principles which it follows transcend all the limits of experience and therefore withdraw themselves from all experimental tests. It is the battle-field of these endless controversies which is called Metaphysic."[2]

Like pure reason, Nature inheres in everything, just as Judeo-Christianity insists that God is everywhere. Again, I am prompted to consider whether there is any essential difference between the reverence—the Jain understatement—and worship—the West's most intrusive verb. Semantically, the intrusion would seem to divide, rather than unite, as history has painfully recorded. By worship, we single one out from among many. By reverence, we mean to apply more generously our admiration. So it is best to recognize that the Jains argue against the opiate of worship for much the reason Karl Marx did: the theology and semantics of worship tend to sunder the heart, the reasoning faculty, even our ability as conscious, loving beings, to consciously love in perpetuity.

Conscious love—the striving towards an harmonious co-existence with all Beings—is the purposeful, soul-supportive, evolutionary instinct of Nature. That, say the Jains, *is* nature. And no semantic penchant, no logical argument, no linquistic or conceptual conquest can do better than that, however it is phrased. Humanity must recognize its place in the natural process. Nature is not something to be worshipped, not some Other; it is ourselves, in need of nurturance and recognition. Short of that, we are not ourselves. We perish as individuals. And as individuals perish, the entire biological community fragments, endures pain. Pain, say the Jains, is unnecessary. And they have shown us how to avoid it.

This is a revolutionary notion. It goes on to insist that human beings are like an island of conscience in a sea of turmoil. We have the capability, the responsibility, to protect one another. For the Jains, "one another" means every organism, living or dead, in the galaxy.

Yet to become a Jain requires far more than mere "reverence" for nature, which is the temptation when describing this common-sense orthodoxy. The Jains recognize in their way that reverence is easy, because it is so identifiable with heaven. Anybody can go to heaven. But it takes courage to remain here on Earth. Neither to ignore, nor forget; but to embrace, and to conquer. Jainism derives from the word *jina*, which means peaceful conquerer; conquerer of one's inner distractions and temptations.

Every religion assists adepts in an addiction to heaven; every psychotherapy calculates its gain by the notches of paradise, the mental tranquility, the ideological utopia it can invent. Paradise is easy. Politicians are forever promising it. Great artists in their passion are invoking it. The Garden of Eden, in other words, is an idea everywhere about us. Yet the actions that should be concomitant with paradise are rare. Indeed, what should they be? For the Jains, this Earth, with its multitudes of life forms and atoms, is the only true sphere of meaning, the place of dreams, of action, of moral and aesthetic culmination. They call it *Jivan-mukhta*, the divine on Earth. But all of these phrases fail to reach the inner soul of Jainism.

There the dimension of thought and behavior can be simply identified by a word, namely, *ahimsa*, which is Hindi for non-violence.

Serving the Jain commonality of purpose, twenty-four exemplary adherents of *ahimsa* are acknowledged to have achieved the bliss of perfect understanding and action. The Jains call them Jinas, or Tirthankaras. They are not gods, but men (and one woman); they did not go to heaven, per se, but to immortal Earth, their souls richly enshrined somewhere in the planet's immortal biochemistry. To call it the summit of a sacred mountain (i.e. Mount Su-Meru or Kailasha in Tibet), or Nirvana, is to cultivate the hieratic inexactitude of yearning beyond all encapsulation, of language that cannot hope to fix between its letters the appropriate physical or emotional coordinates. For the Jains, topography becomes relevant when it has entered the Soul.

The most recent of these Jinas, Mahavira, lived in Bihar (eastern India) from 599 to 527 B.C., and was an older contemporary of Gautama Buddha, who knew of him. Both men shared certain qualities—great renunciations, extreme psychological embattlement, unfriendly opponents, legendary hardships. In the case of Mahavira, his abdication of the normal material existence occurred only after his parents had died. He did not want his parents to suffer from missing him. Mahavira took off his clothes and spent some forty years wandering across India preaching the message of peace. He was a total vegetarian and Jainism itself is adamantly so.

Mahavira's nudity (*acelakka*) is well worth commenting upon, for it suggests a state of purity and inner unity that—it must be acknowledged—is rather rare in these times.

There are, however, nearly sixty existing naked Jain monks (*Digambara* sect Jains) in India who spend but a few days at any one time in any one village. They are dependent upon those who will feed them pure vegetarian food—food that is said to possess but one sense: specific fruits, vegetables, grains, and nuts. One meal a day, when they are not fasting, eaten out of the palms of their hands; food which they consume knowing that even the one-sensed organisms, like soy, want to live, want not to be eaten. All Jains, not just the fewer number of white-robed (*Shvetambara*) and naked (*Digambara*) monks, have reduced their consumption, however, to one sense so as not to starve. A human being, like most animals, has five senses. And because Jains are devoted to minimizing violence on this Earth, they recognize that it is better to spare the five-sensed being, even if it means consuming the one-sensed.

Such gradations of behavior are consistent with the Jain philosophy of non-absolutism (*anekantavada*), the relativity of thinking. What is not suited to relativity, however, is the killing or harming of any organism with more than one sense, except in instances of total self-defense, where once again the minimizing of violence as a general principle is employed.

What this means, practically speaking, is that the Jains have renounced all professions involving harm to animals. Not surprisingly, their ecological vocations have proved to be immensely successful financially and the Jain communities throughout India find themselves economically advantaged. They have used their money philanthropically to perpetuate the practice of *ahimsa*. They have established animal welfare centers known as *panjorapors*, compassionate oases in a harsh country where cattle are beloved to death, in essence; left to wander, in other words, until they typically starve in old age or sooner. Jains once again interfere with nature, rescuing the old or infirm animals and caring for them lovingly until they die natural deaths inside the sanctuaries.

The Jains always granted equal status to women. There was never a caste system among the Jains. How could there be? Abortion and contraception are allowed, though abortion itself is not religiously sanctioned. Here again, where the mother's own physical or mental well-being is jeopardized, her adulthood is granted priority status. Pragmatic minimizing of violence is once again at work.

Agricultural professions, timber, even mineral exploitation, most pharmaceutical or any earth-moving enterprises—these are all outside the Jain level of comfort. Hotels which serve non-vegetarian food to their guests are also in opposition to every Jain canon. Jain doctors cannot prescribe any drugs that derived from animal by-products, or were ever tested on animals. Jain lawyers are vehemently opposed to any form of physical punishment. Jains stay out of the military unless called upon to defend the nation during an active conflict. Jains even forego silk saris, so fundamental to pan-Indian fashion, knowing as they do that appoximately 10,000 silk worms are boiled alive to make a single garment. As for Jain monks, they are celibate, but not for the reasons non-sexuality has been ordained in other religious quarters. For the Jain mendicants, ejaculation is perceived in stark terms: it kills, on average, 75 million spermatazoa, while wreaking havoc with the bacterial balance of a woman's genitalia.

Once again, however, lay Jains propagate themselves in spite of these uncomfortable recognitions, always oriented in their hearts toward that day when they too can renounce sex, renounce automobiles (cars kill bugs), and simply walk naked, barefoot, throughout their homeland, gently brushing insects out of their path, avoiding stepping on grass, practicing the primary rules of *ahimsa*.

Rules are basic to Jain ecology. They translate into daily practices that are meant to inhibit the unrestrained inflow of quotidian sensation, passion, *karma*. Karma covers the soul, say the Jains, the way a cataract clouds and inhibits the vision. The goal of the Jain is to restrict, and eventually banish the accumulation of karma—material goods, passions, ill-will towards others, complexity, haste, narcissism, ego in all its phases—so that the soul can be free of inconsequential attachments and harmful deeds. They call this condition *kshayika-samyak-darshana*, translated as "true insight through the destruction of karma." When that day comes, a Jain will have achieved his *moksha*, or liberation.

Jains have their own form of Ten Commandments (the five *anuvratas* or vows). These major convictions consist of *ahimsa* (non-violence—with literally hundreds of psychoanalyzed forms of behavior to avoid or to embrace), *satya* (truth), *asteya* (not stealing), *brahmacarya* (sexual abstinence) and *aparigraha* (non-possession). In addition, there are eleven *pratimas*—stages of spiritual progress; and eight *mulagunas*, the basic restraints.

In negotiating their way through this labyrinth of injunctions, the lay Jains strive towards monkhood. Few actually achieve that state of complete itinerant renunciation, best articulated, perhaps, by a naked Digambara who once sat with me at a temple above the city of Indore and spoke the following words: "Twenty-two years ago I took the vow of nudity. Extraordinary as it may appear to you, nudity has become natural to us…We do not possess anything whatsoever and we do not have to tell people to likewise give up their worldly possessions. Our example itself conveys the fact that here is a man who can be happy without having or wanting anything. It is important to see that what hurts himself also must hurt others and what gives happiness to others alone can give happiness to himself. It is ahimsa that makes for friendship between father and son, and love between husband and wife. With these words I bless you. May the whole world remain in peace."[3]

There is in Jainism a practice of "temporary asceticism," much like a fasting or meditation retreat, which makes a monk out of a businessman for a day, or a weekend, or as long as he or she wishes to emulate the foregoing convictions.

I have spent considerable time in India in this mode of impermanent austerity, or *tapas*. But it is a mistake to assume that Asia is where ascetics can best manage. India is *not* the essential ingredient of such behavior. Jain awareness is what matters. And it is as appropriate in the U.N. General Assembly or the World Court at the Hague, as it is on Wall Street, or in Hollywood or Washington. The space of this meditation never ceases, never need change. A café in downtown Tokyo, the sculptured caverns of ancient Ellora. In a marble enclave atop a high Maharastran tropic, or on a drowsy train headed to nowhere, across Siberia. Whatever the personal circumstances of time or place, the same cacophany of senses is rushing in to proclaim the Earth herself as the basis for humble and reverential thought and deed. Jainism can work in the industrial sections of Manchester, England, or in a place like Ahmedabad, along a sleepy Gujarati river, where Gandhi spent many years spinning his own fabric, meditating, building a case against the British occupation of India, and practicing the Jainism which his earliest mentor, a Jain teacher, and his closest friend, a Jain ascetic, had inculcated in the Mahatma.

"If ahimsa be not the law of our being, then my whole argument falls to pieces," wrote Gandhi.

Jainism can work, and must work, anywhere, everywhere. It is environmental meditation taken to its logical conclusion. Ironically, the Jains within India have become remarkably adept capitalists. Though they collectively account for but one percent of India's nearly one billion residents, they pay a proportionate lion's share of the country's taxes, as well as providing the overwhelming majority of philanthropic donations. Their ecological professions have proven to be among the most lucrative enterprises: businesses like law, computer software, publishing, education, diamond cutting, the judiciary, administration, and so forth. None of these activities would be considered altogether pure by the Jain monks, of course. Diamond cutting, for example, disturbs the inorganic balance of the planet, not so much on the finger of one's bride, but in the deep and unrestrained shafts where the diamonds are rudely hewn. Publishing is even more injurious, for the obvious reasons. A single edition of a newspaper in Bombay, regardless of the amount of recycled pulp, has taken its devastating toll on the forests and the surrounding ecosystem.

Nevertheless, the Jains have gone a remarkable distance in minimizing their impact, by comparison with most of their contemporary humans.

And what I was to discover in my various encounters with new Jain friends is the stunning extent to which they are constantly attuned to, and talking about a meditation on nature, simplification, the largesse which is appropriate to human conscience.

Environmental meditation, according to the Jain approach, seeks to meld the Earth with all that is personal and evocative. That is to say, something large has become something small; a whole planet has been incorporated into the germ of an ideal.

That the Jains have qualified their ecological thinking by reference to the unconscious and to rudimentary psychology, suggests the level of concern they share for understanding the roots of human aggression and the possibilities for reversing those tendencies inside a person.

By psychoanalyzing violence, breaking down daily *himsa*, or harm, into its minute parts, the Jains have discovered the wellspring of compassion. At every juncture of human behavior they have divined right and wrong, signaling hope, allowing for gentleness, finding a path towards love that is viable, humble, appropriate to everyone. The *dharma-tirtha*, or holy path, is the result of daily salutations (*namaskara-mantra*), compassion, empathy and charity (*jiva-daya*), care in walking (*irya-samiti*), forgiveness (*kshama*), universal friendliness (*maitri*), affirmation (*astikya*), the sharing with guests (*atithi-samvibhaga*), critical self-examination (*alocana*), behavioral restraints (*gunavratas*), aversion leading to renunciation (*vairagya*), and constant meditation on these matters (*dhyana*). These many assertions of a daily quest, taken together, are the basis for liberation in this life, the realization that all souls are interdependent (*parasparopagraho jivanam*).

Mahavira had stated: "One who neglects or disregards the existence of earth, air, fire, water and vegetation disregards his own existence which is entwined with them." But the ideal goes far beyond biology. The fact of fickle evolution is no excuse for bad behavior. Evolution does not condemn us to anything. Our choices condemn us. We are not clouds in trousers, drifting out of control, but forces for empathy, capable of adroit and systematic deliberation. As Thoreau cautioned, we must live our lives deliberately. Such that the very ecological ground rules that have surfaced in this century are now seen to have the same origins many millennia ago of a cultural and spiritual phenomenon known as Jainism. When Mahavira gave his first sermon, his audience was called by him *Samavasarana*, meaning, a congregation of people and all other animals, even snakes and scorpions and insects.[4] A Puddleby-on-Marsh of universal sensibility.

Consider the insect, any insect: a bumble bee stranded in wet sand, on some beach, somewhere, inexplicably urging itself towards oblivion. You have seen it. Or have come across other dying remnants of a mysterious pattern in nature. Or is it a pattern? The rational mind presumes much about evolution and the everyday. If it is happening, there must be a rule which makes it so; a scientific calculation which holds that this is not the first bumble bee to drown itself or the first gazelle to be brought down by a cheetah.

And so there is a temptation to let it be, which Jainism has—for thousands of years—advocated. To let nature take its course, in other words, and not interfere. But there is a second, at times contradictory layer of Jain thinking which states unambiguously, "A wise person should not act sinfully towards earth, nor cause others to act so, nor allow others to act so."[5]

It is this latter exhortation—"nor allow others"—that requires especial consideration. For the Jains, then, ecology and meditation are one and the same; an Earth in the Self that becomes, again, the Earth. The concept is a concept, but it is also a revolutionary (though self-evident) form of action; a realm given to the identifying and solving of misgivings, imbalance, trauma, sadness. Ecological activism that is introspectional; contemplation that is extroverted.

Jain ecology is thus a process of bringing the whole world of nature—of all life—into the inner Being. There, the focus of *samayika*, of restraint in meditation and action, blossoms into an embrace of the utter life principle which is the Earth and all of her interdependent, interrelational beings. In samayika, those relations are fused into an understanding of the self. The complexity of this fusion, ecologically speaking, can be understood in any number of important ways. For example, when one species of tree goes extinct in the tropics, dozens, possibly even hundreds of animal species are likely to go extinct with it. We may chop down a tree and say, "In all humility, I have chopped down only one tree to build a simple cabin for myself." Or, we may acknowledge that to chop down that tree is to cause unimaginable harm. This is the contradiction inherent to the human psyche. The opponents are clearly delineated in Jainism. And the soul, the *jiva*, is its battleground.

According to the Jains, every soul in every organism, is an individual, with a dream, a want, a fervent hope. All organisms feel pain. No one wants to suffer, neither the bacteria in one's armpit, the 36,000 cubic feet of life in a redwood tree, nor the child. We are all individuals, to repeat: beings with souls; beings with needs. And we must be allowed to evolve according to our own inner energies. Thus, the Jains have sought to protect the wildness in everyone; to reinstate the dignity and original purpose of the wilderness; to reconnect with the nature in everything.

To argue, as many have done, that animals and insects kill one another, a contention often set forth to justify human meat-eating habits, is to ignore the great Jain calling which recognizes violence in the world but vehemently insists that human beings and other animals as well, have the ability to reverse the pernicious in nature; to forge a new evolutionary standard; to celebrate and coddle, love and nurture. And it is thus our responsibility to do so; to make *loving*, not killing, the preferred medium of exchange on Earth. We can do it, say the Jains. And I believe them.

In one of their many stories, it is said that Mahavira, in a former life, was a lion who—upon speaking with a Jain monk—resolved to die of hunger rather than harm any other living being, and upon his death, was immediately reborn the 24th Tirthankara.

We may well pass on without having learned many answers, but the same questions of a life force with which Jainism is pre-eminently concerned will always prevail. Such questions concern the universal decency, and the possibilities for joy and empathy which are our responsibility to engender, as compassionate, rational individuals confronted by a sea of tumultuous evolution.

The soul of Jainism is thus about stewardship, requiring human diligence, human conscience and human love. Jain ecology is nothing more than universal love (*mettim bhavehi*). [6]

And it is this quality which ensures that the Jains are not merely insular success stories, saving a ghetto here, a neighborhood there, while the larger world collapses all around them. Quite to the contrary, the Jains have indeed embraced the whole planet with their passionate idealism.

The bumble bee, like the tree, is on a path. It has an individual soul, obviously; a desire; an inclination; a hope. What am I to do? Leave the bumble bee alone, as I would leave the tree alone? The question requires no belaboring. Do unto others as you would have them do unto you. This is fundamental Jainism. Or, more accurately, this is fundamental humanity, what Aristotle likened to the *summum bonum* of human aspiration.

Some will argue that I have altered time, space, history, *dharma*, the law, by saving the bee. But to ignore my feelings would be to alter my own dharma, my destiny, which bids me to carefully lift the bee onto a finger and trek the beach in search of green plants and fresh water. I wash off the sand that has stuck to the bee's eyes, then set her down in shade, where there are no evident predators. Am I making a mistake? Keeping her from depositing eggs on the seashore like a turtle, or presenting herself to a dreamed-of afterlife in the ocean? Possibly, though she is no queen bee and no turtle, and she appeared stuck in the sand, dying and in pain.

At least now she has the chance to live and resume her life.

To many, such activities reflect mere sentimentality, stupidity or intense anthropomorphism. Maybe, maybe not. I only know that I feel something for the bee; more than something, I feel like that bee. I am that bee. I too am stuck in the sand, just to have seen it, to have imagined its predicament, and the fear of a giant shadow stepping towards it, cupping it in its claw (mine) and lifting it dozens and dozens of inches upwards toward the free sky, toward the cloud of unknowing.

All of us have been that bumble bee, certainly. All of us will be so again.

The continuity of need, of the realization of peril and of the imperative of love, are the first intuitions of Jainism. Collectively, the word is *ahimsa*. But beyond the word there is an entire lifetime of love to give, love to feel, a whole world to bring inside the body and meditate upon.

Once the meditation—the summoning of feeling—has been started, there is no turning back.

"Khamemi sabbajive
sabbe jiva khamantu me
metti me sabbabhuyesu
veram majjha na kenavi."

(The words of a Digambara monk, spoken to the author, meaning, "I forgive all beings, may all beings forgive me. I have friendship toward all, malice toward none." [7]

[1]Excerpt from the teachings of the Jinas, in *Religion and Culture Of The Jains*, by Dr. Jyoti Prasad Jain, p. 187, Bharatiya Jnanpith Publication, New Delhi, 1983.

[2]Immanuel Kant's *Critique Of Pure Reason*, translated by F. Max Müller, xvii-xviii, Macmillan Company, London, 1896. A different approach to the same problem can be found in the following statement of the 11th century Chinese philosopher, Ch'eng I, "All things in the world can be understood in the light of reason. Each entity works according to its principle or the order of nature. In each, therefore, there is reason. Human nature is reason." From *The Development of Neo-Confucian Thought*, by Carsun Chang, pp. 211, 217, Bookman Associates, New York 1957.

[3]Translated at the Digambara Temple above Indore in January, 1986, by P. S. Jaini, consultant to the author's PBS film, *Ahimsa: Non-violence*.

[4]op. cit., J. P. Jain, p.15.

[5]The words of the 24th Tirthankara, or Jina, Mahavira, quoted from the *Acaranga Sutra*, one of the most ancient and important religious texts of Jainism. The fuller text reads, "As somebody may cut or strike a blind man (who cannot see the wound), as somebody may cut or strike the foot, the ankle, the knee, the thigh, the hip, the navel, the belly, the flank, the back, the bosom, the heart, the breast, the neck, the arm, the finger, the nail, the eye, the brow, the forehead, the head, as some kill (openly), as some

extirpate (secretly), (thus the earth-bodies are cut, struck, and killed though their feeling is not manifest). He who injures these (earth-bodies) does not comprehend and renounce the sinful acts; he who does not injure these, comprehends and renounces the sinful acts. Knowing them, a wise man should not act sinfully towards earth, nor cause others to act so, nor allow others to act so. He who knows these causes of sin relating to earth, is called a reward-knowing sage. Thus I say." pp. 4-5, "The Akaranga Sutra," Book I, Lecture I, Lesson 3, in *Jaina Sutras*, translated from Prakrit by Hermann Jacobi, Motilal Banarsidass, New Delhi, 1980; first published by Oxford University Press, 1884.

[6]See *Asceticism In Ancient India*, by Haripada Chakraborti, Punthi Pustak Publishing, Calcutta, 1973, pp. 423, 425.

[7]Translated by Dr. Padmanabh S. Jaini, University of California-Berkeley, in his essay, "*Ahimsa: A Jaina Way of Personal Discipline*," p. 21. See also the book *Life Force : The World of Jainism*, by Michael Tobias, Asian Humanities Press, Berkeley, 1991.

V
On Behalf of Animals

These are they which follow the Lamb withersoever he goeth.

—from the *Revelation of Saint John the Divine*[1]

The meditation on non-violence and harmony must lead from the inner soul to the universal soul in order to be fulfilled and true. All organisms are endowed with a soul. The resulting equation becomes self-evident with even the most fleeting inward reflection.

No religion, no ethical particularity, no logic, no scientific argument, need be advanced in order to justify the abhorrence that I—and I can't even imagine how many others—have against the exploitation of animals. As human organisms, so-called, we are endowed with a conscience, a delicate spark of empathy, as the ancient Greeks likened it (*synderesis* was their word). This quality of mind and soul exists, theoretically, like some safe harbor in a sea teeming with pirates.

That very conscience has been increasingly benumbed, however, by cultural decree; by scientific myth and brazen denial.

For example, take the erroneous assertion that we are the product of a meat-eating evolution. There is ample scientific evidence to counter this attitude (which is all it is), but I find a recourse to logic more revealing. There is no residual biology in my gut that commands me to involuntarily slay the neighborhood grocer for my food, any more than it commands people in general to kill a cow. To suggest the analogy that lions and ants kill, and therefore people can kill with a clear conscience (inasmuch as nature seems to have ordained such killing), has already taken the meat-eating argument out of the realm of physical anthropology and into the arena of opinion and taste. Taste, a constantly changing chemistry of a few nerve endings in the tongue, is nothing more than a personal matter, as unfixed as the fashions one chooses to wear or the books one reads.

It is known that most, if not all, of recent human evolution was accompanied by fire, the impact of fire on the evolving neo-cortex[2], in addition to the hybridization of wild grains in the Near East allowing for the first stable agriculture. Meat had nothing to do with human progress, though much to do with its isolation from the animal community and its own sexual dsyfunctionalism. The slaughter of animals made the taking of slaves and the conquest of the female more congenial to certain males. When Claude-Levi Strauss makes the point that the difference between people and all other animals is the difference between the cooked and the raw, he is not asserting that cooking is what *makes* a person, only what distinguishes him. What makes a person, I suspect, is the complexion of his conscience.

It was in the Near East some 60,000 years ago, at the Caves of Shanidar in the Zagros Mounains of northern Iraq, that one of the earliest documented acts of conscience comes to light. An injured resident was surgically operated upon, his shoulder set straight (probably the victim of rock fall). That same individual died shortly thereafter and was buried with a tiara of wildflowers on his head. His grave was adorned with other flowering species. This was a time of vegetarianism on Earth; when the big game hunters in southern Spain were virtually out-of-business. Most of the million or so Homo erectus and later Neanderthal and Cro-Magnons survived on pulses, tubers, nuts, berries and wild fruits, gathered by the women and children and probably quite a few of the men. Shanks of mastodon were rare and infrequent additions to a diet that suffered no need of additional protein.

Clearly, there is abominable pain throughout the wilderness. But it is equally true that people can act day by day, moment by moment, to alleviate pain, to minimize cruelty, to stop hunting and killing and hurting right now, this moment. And can control that whimsy, those taste buds, which continue to indulge the spoils of other anonymous killers conveniently arrayed at grocery stores. Those killers, today, include major multinational corporations. The largest of them, based in Amarillo, Texas, "processes" nearly six billion large mammals every year. The killing is done crudely, by young men and women whose job description entails only two things, that they be good with knives, and not mind walking knee-deep in the blood of loving creatures that have been brutally slaughtered, in absence of any conscience whatsoever; or of any implemented laws.

Isn't the alleviation of suffering the basis upon which family values—that expression given political loft in the 1990s—rest? It is the vow taken by all doctors in their profession. The reasons saints have been canonized, Nobel Prizes in Peace and Medicine awarded. The very behavior of an Albert Schweitzer or Mother Theresa whose courage has been cited as reminders to our children of what they should strive for.

Millions of animal species are going extinct, not because lions kill gazelles and ants devour grasshoppers, but because human beings kill wantonly, indifferently, and in ways that destroy whole ecosystems.

I hear countless lightweight pieces of diatribe over the right, the need, the rationale for and against hunting and meat-eating. But nowhere do I see meatpackers, hunters or environmentalists, philosophers, or theologians debating the most simple and pervasive of all edicts—the one we all grew up with, Buddhist, Jew, Christian, Native American, Jain, Muslim, Hindu, Taoist, Australasian, Native African, Aborigine, or Martian, for that matter, namely, that "Thou Shalt Not Kill."

There is no debate over the wisdom of the Ten Commandments. The power of this document as well as its collective reasoning is self-evident. And this is the overwhelming, unambiguous consensus that must prevail if this miraculous planet of life is to prosper. No ifs, ands, or buts. No debate is necessary. The message is clear. It needs only to be re-formulated as an amendment to the Constitution; a wide-ranging provision for animals.

If every child were taught not to kill, if every adult remembered not to kill, under any circumstances, if the pain and suffering everywhere inherent to nature could impress human nature, which so prides itself on having evolved the ability to choose, to make thoughtful decisions, then the killing would cease.

This is not about the rights of hunters and meat-eaters. This is not about the constitutional right of people to carry arms—a right that would become anachronistic in light of the new animal amendment, I suspect. This is about the special gift that human beings possess in their hearts, in their souls…the gift of gift-giving.

The gift comes from individuals, not movements or nation states. We exchange vows. We exchange love. We love to give gifts. Birthday gifts. Wedding gifts and anniversary gifts. Gifts and cards on every imaginable occasion. Why not give the gift of life to animals?

Don't hinge the argument on preservation, on conservation. Hunters would like people to believe that they are staunch conservationists. They want to preserve ducks in order to shoot their brains out, in other words. But, in fact, duck populations in the last thirty-five years have declined disastrously. According to the EPA, between 1955 and 1986, mallard populations in the U.S. had declined by forty percent, black ducks and pintails by sixty percent. Both as a result of hunting, as well as the sorry fact that America's wetlands are being destroyed at a rate of nearly 300,000 acres every year.[3]

Furthermore, conservation is not the appropriate noun to utilize when referring to animals. Animals—all of us—are not mere resources. We are not numbers. We are living beings with unique destinies and souls; able to feel, to imagine, to think, to speak. We are all animals.

Just the other night, during an intermission of *Der Rosenkavalier*, following the superb little waltz at the end of Act II, my wife happened upon a sluggish Rhinocerous beetle enjoying the music and the warmth of the concrete aisle, still warm from the daylight. She lifted it to safety only to receive a verbal thrashing from the little creature which apparently did not want to move. I was not present for this William Burroughs-like display, but it clearly had a grand impact on my wife, who could think of nothing but that adroit two-inch long linguist throughout Act III of the Strauss opera.

How did it sound, what did it say, I asked her?

It grumbled hysterically, like a cantankerous old grandma with arthritis, she indicated.

The point being, even insects are not necessarily what they appear to be. To quote from Shakespeare's *Twelfth Night*, "Thou shalt hold the opinion of Pythagoras, ere I will allow of thy wits; and fear to kill a woodcock, lest thou dispossess the soul of thy granddam."

We are all subject to frequent reincarnation, what in Greece was likened to the soul's transmigration, and what throughout India is termed *samsara*. But because human beings have the ability to desist, to exercise the megatonnage, the throw-weight of conscience, it is up to us to uphold a sense of decorum on Earth.

Forget the arguments, the debates, the legal, economic and scientific points of view—some flimsy, some penetrating; let go of the verbiage, rancor and tired platitudes. Own up to the one gentle message of non-violence.

In the early 17th century, a famed Japanese Shogun, Ieyasu, decided he, too, had seen enough hunting and killing of all kinds by the several million samurai of his day. He imposed a ban on all killing. He forbade the making of guns, which had recently been introduced by the Portuguese to his country. And, for the following 225 years, Japan was relatively quiet. Historians have remarked that those two centuries represent the most sustained period of peace in any land that the civilized world has ever known.

A thousand years before Ieyasu, a Japanese Fujiwara Emperor had signed into law the liberation of all Japanese house pets and animals of toil.

In Medieval India, the Moghul ruler Akhbar—out of deference to a Jain mendicant—outlawed the killing of any animals in India during those days particularly holy to the Jains.

In Sweden, recent bovine legislation has made it illegal to keep cows in pens. They must be free to wander in open pasture.

In the state of Rajasthan, Jain politicians have managed to persuade the government to forbid the butchering of animals several days each year. If all butchering and meat-eating were halted for just 24 hours a year in the United States, some twenty million animals' deaths would be at least postponed.

In other words, even in piecemeal increments, there are precedents for believing that the human collective, guided by conscience, can transcend society's habitual fall into violence.

Killing is not fixed in our genes. Empathy is. Humor is. Child-rearing is. Positiveness is. We may be Hegelians, dwelling on thesis and antithesis; indwelling on doom and gloom; but it is incumbent upon us to focus on synthesis, on upbeat endings, happiness, if only for the sake of our children and their children. Otherwise, we are part of the problem, to recite the truism.

We are fickle. But fickleness, like evolution, need not be implacable. And no dietary explanation can be offered in support of bad habits.

Even supposedly deep thinkers have collapsed over the issue of our humanity. Consider Ortega y Gasset, otherwise noted for his study of the dehumanization of the masses. In his book, *Meditation On Hunting*, y Gasset has written, "When one is hunting the air has another, more exquisite feel as it glides over the skin or enters the lungs; the rocks acquire a more expressive physiognomy, and the vegetation becomes loaded with meaning. All this is due to the fact that the hunter, while he advances or waits crouching, feels tied through the earth to the animal he pursues."

Philosophers or fools, fickle or not, we have to learn. We must stop inflicting our muscle-man mentality; we have to wake up. Killing is wrong. The largest animal that ever lived, the most powerful—the brontosaurus— was vegetarian. Elephants, gorillas, and the largest shark in the world, the megamouth, are also vegetarians. One may wish to debate the fine points: yes, lettuce has feeling, as the Jains have so accurately pointed out. But the bottom line is the *minimizing* of pain. A cow has more of an ability to feel than lettuce. I don't know that for certain, of course; I just have a hunch. Clarence Darrow's summation in the Leopold-Loeb trial of the 1920's made it clear that bloodlust does not satisfy anybody or any principle, in the end. Affected by the reasonableness of his argument, the judge set down a sentence of life imprisonment, though the climate of the times vigorously called for the young men's executions.

Sometimes it comes down to whose pain is greater: the mother who does not want, or cannot physically endure her pregnancy, or the rights of an unborn fetus, in the case of abortion; the survivors, or the comatose victim, in the case of euthanasia. Hunters argue that killing off "excess game" prevents those animals in question from starving to death, and is therefore a form of mercy killing. But no life form can or should ever be described as "excess game." The indignity, the wrongness of it strikes at the bone of any feeling person. Would one condone the killing off of "excess" Somalians during a time of famine? No. The impulse is, and must be, care, help, provision. We are not judges and executioners. Nature has that job. We are shepherds by dint of our power and our hearts. Hunting, and thus meat-eating (a unity too easily overlooked), is a throw-back to a primitive time when our hearts were more callous. When we were, in fact, different animals.

Today is the beginning. Start now. Forget what has transpired. Put down your weapons. There is no ill-feeling. No reason to perpetuate the past. Simply an urgency that grows more fervent by the minute and is called the future. The need to become peaceful, to stop the killing. To abolish not just hunting, of course, but all behavior which kills, or harms, or exploits animals—all animals—in any way. When will an independent presidential candidate have the wisdom and the courage to run on a vegetarian ticket? When will a congressman recognize that animals are entitled to the same legal standing as humans? That anything short of this (i.e., the obscenely inadequate Animal Welfare Act) is a fatal flaw in the integrity and longevity of any democracy? As Gandhi once stated, the truth of any supposedly civilized people can only be determined by its treatment of animals.

What would it feel like to live in this country if the unbearable shame of our colossal abuse of animals were to be lifted? What pathological reprieve, in the air, between all people, a lightness like the sun and the moon; a blue sky, a melody, a return to an unimaginable Eden of joy and compassion and freedom? If only the consumer was not handfed his own degradation; encouraged to fall back perpetually into old habits? Habits of destruction and self-destruction? Patterns of hate and apathy that have traumatized nearly every child—and thus every adult—that was ever born into an American household? A syndrome of vengeance, of repudiation, of machismo and weakness that has violated every canon of humanity by which our species was ever meant to be judged?

A constitutional amendment on behalf of animals, that's what I am proposing. Local canvassing, national lobbying, community gatherings, school agendas, church synods and national conventions. A political revolution that would endeavor to find leaders and draw up legislation to put the meat, seafood and poultry industries out-of-business forever. To ensure that not one more hamburger ever be produced or sold in North America. That never another crab or lobster, dolphin or whale, seal or salmon, tuna or halibut be captured. Legislation that would abolish all biomedical research; that would make zoos—like hamburgers—bizarre aberrations of the past; and put an end to horse and dog racing, the use of animals in the film industry and in any kind of circus; that would liberate unhappy pets and close down all pet stores; that would criminalize the possession of bullets and cages, butterfly nets and hunting knives, and make all animals—beetles, bears, rabbits, goats, horses, monkeys, chipmunks, bats, deer, bison, moose, chickens, cows, fish, ants, sheep, pigs, elephants, children, moms, dads, single women, single men, and any others you care to name—national treasures, subject to the will of no man, and beholden for their existence to no sudden economic expedient, aesthetic vogue, or moment of moral arrogance. A nation of inviolate Beings, one and all, great and small.

Laws to protect other life forms just as we have endeavored to safeguard historical monuments, the rights of mass murderers, museums, drug informants, national parks, and animals of all sorts inhabiting the Oval Office.

Legislation, finally, that would abolish all artificial human controls on animal populations; cease the manufacture of fishing poles, pesticides and bug sprays of any kind. That would let the animals run wild and name the turkey as our national bird. One that we would feed and love, not eat.

There are probably one or two ethical and practical concerns that would have to be worked out. That would not be difficult. The animals would help us find a way. But in the end, recalling Gandhi's pronouncement that the British are going to walk out, the Americans are going to seek forgiveness. What we need, during the transition, is to set aside tens of millions of acres as preserves for all the animals rescued from American callousness. To re-establish migratory and feeding corridors—whether for bison in Montana, whooping cranes between Nebraska and Louisiana, or frogs in Hawaii.

To transform American oblivion into American compassion. To end, finally, the torture and slaughter of well over ten billion North American mammals every year, and far more avians and rodents and insects.

The actual task of saving animals, of altering the diet of over 200 million American humans (there are an estimated 40 million existing vegetarians in the U.S.), of closing down quite a few industries, changing others (such as the animal bashing by car makers), transforming the medical and pharmaceutical supply conglomerates, as well as the way medical students are indoctrinated and researchers funded; of filing an avalanche of class action suits on behalf of animals under the new legislation, and thus, of training a whole new generation of animal and plant defense lawyers, would surely kindle a renaissance in consciousness. Other nations, economically tied to the American way, would surely follow. There would be, at first, a surge of entrepreneurial opportunism in heavy meat-eating countries like England, China, Argentina, Germany and Thailand. But without the American consumer to encourage it, all that blood money would eventually be diverted towards humane profits. New job training would result; new types of jobs. An animal corps of engineers, vegetarian one and all, schooled in the philosophies of Mahavira, Aldo Leopold, St. Francis and the paleolithic goddesses of lore, would be employed to manage the task, in part. There would be jobs aplenty.

And there would be money aplenty as well. Why? Because a vegetarian America would no longer allow for a 250 billion dollar annual defense budget. Because a vegetarian America would suffer far fewer meat and heavy cholesterol-dependent diseases—as John Robbins has admirably described, in his book, *Diet For A New America*; because a nation which returned its produce directly to the people, as opposed to food bins to fatten cattle and swine, would have less monoculture and a good deal more water. Keep in mind that only one percent of all water on Earth is fresh water; that the majority of that one percent is now polluted; and that most of what's finally left in the United States is used to grow alfalfa for hog and cattle feed. The meat industry is an ecological disaster. Once weaned away from a meat diet, the American economy, the American landscape, and overweight Americans, in general, would witness a spectacular revival while cattle ranches in Latin America which have usurped the tropical rain forests, will find fewer and fewer markets for their meat.[4]

But most importantly of all, America's psyche would be rid—not of its past—but of its existing demons. And that is a beginning for *all* animals.[5]

What can I do? What can you do? Begin by sparing the spider nestled in the corner of your ceiling. Check your bathtub or shower before you turn on the water. Remember that the presence of insects in your home is a good omen. The presence of animals in your path, or overhead, is a sign that you are being protected. To think kindly of another animal places you in good fellowship with all earth spirits. To actually care for other animals is the beginning of happiness. To eat and think peacefully is to begin to feel the joy of creation. To walk lightly. To tower above and beyond the petty cruelties of life, and to be a new person, a new and powerful being, endowed with grace and wisdom. This is the secret source of longevity: a soul that has never killed will never die.

[1] *The Revelation of Saint John the Divine*, Foreward by Ernest H. Short, p. 134, Philip Allan & Co. Edition, London 1926.

[2] See the chapters on fire in the author's books, *After Eden - History, Ecology & Conscience*, Avant Books, 1985, and *Voice of the Planet*, Bantam Books, 1990.

[3] See "America On The Edge," by Tom Huth, *Traveler*, September 1992, p. 138.

[4] See Debra Blake Weisenthal's "Do You Have A Planet-Healthy Diet?" pp. 42-47, *Vegetarian Times*, Issue 180, August 1992. Weisenthal highlights the recommendations of nutritionist Joan Dye Gussow whose philosophy of conscientious eating takes into account the loss of genetic diversity resulting from the monocropping, crop diseases and soil loss associated with what is essentially cattle fed corn. In addition, Wesienthal points to Gussow's contention that "most of our saturated fat and all our cholesterol intake come from animal products." Even the U.S. Department of Agriculture, in its recent "seven" guidelines, has begun to recognize this fact.

[5] A portion of this essay is adapted from the author's article, "Thou Shalt Not Kill," *Trilogy Magazine*, November/December 1991, pp. 90-92.

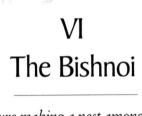

VI
The Bishnoi

The vulture making a nest among the rocks
Is the sign that his life-force will be harder than rock.

—Tsang Nyon Heruka[1]

In the deserts of western India, the nearly one million Bishnoi have lived as non-violent vegetarians for hundreds of years, unaffected by perpetual drought. Like the Jains, these soft-spoken Hindus have elevated meditation to a practical science that could alleviate human suffering throughout much of the developing world.

In 1988, my wife Jane and I trekked across an arid swathe of mirages and dust back into an esoteric time, in search of a rumored cultural bridge between the spiritual Middle Ages and an ecologically attuned future. We went in search of an important secret, into the heart of the Tar desert, a vast and desolate region in India's western state of Rajasthan.

Nearly three million Hindus, Sikhs, Muslims and Bishnoi, along with nine million cattle, sheep, goats, water buffalo and camels, inhabit this flat and desiccated wilderness. Typically, any given year witnesses between 25 and 60 centimeters of rainfall in this region. But the total annual rainfall for the period 1983 to 1988 was a mere one centimeter, amounting to the worst drought ever recorded in western India, where most populations are already living on the edge.

Hundreds of millions of Indians depend upon the crops which are watered by the summer monsoons. But, as of 1986, even the Indian press was acknowledging the fact that at least 100 million Indians were suffering from malnutrition because the monsoons had failed. In the Indian Ocean, water at the surface was a few degrees cooler than usual, so the rain fell over the sea before reaching the land. Or that was one hypothesis. Perhaps it was because of global warming, or vast volcanic effluents somewhere else, or the result of some other unknown meteorological anomaly tied to human pollution.

Famine affected most of the 27 districts in Rajasthan when the monsoons failed. Herders took their cattle across the border to Pakistan to sell them at any price. Government officials were predicting the worst famine in India's history. That was in 1986. Two years later, when my wife and I were there, the drought was worsening and people were dying.

Throughout Rajasthan we visited the funeral pyres, huge heaps of dead cattle at road junctures, teeming with grateful vultures. Everywhere were scattered the bleached and aching bones of creatures that had perished. A 500 square kilometer graveyard. At least 35 percent of the cattle—the primary means of subsistence for most of the communities in the area—had expired from hunger and dehydration.

But what about those few districts which seemed, remarkably, to manage in spite of disaster?

S. M. Mohnot, a professor of zoology at Jodhpur University, was a soft-spoken gentleman who had organized 100 environmentalists on an 800 kilometer journey by foot throughout drought-ridden Rajasthan earlier that year. He had walked with the scientists from village to village to assess conditions and explore any local measures to counter continuing conditions. Mohnot served as the environmental adviser to the Bishnoi, a community of a million people, a handsome, buoyantly dressed sub-sect of the Hindus. His effort to bring the Bishnoi's extraordinary secret to the attention of other ecologists, policy makers and villagers throughout India gained recognition when, in January of 1988, the Indian government named the Bishnoi village of Khejare as the first National Environmental Memorial to commemorate the death of 363 Bishnoi men, women and children.

As I sat in Mohnot's house one night listening to his tale, before Jane and I had set out ourselves for Bishnoi country, I assumed that he was going to elaborate upon the carnage, one more set of dreary statistics pertaining to the famine. But that was not it.

The fact of 363 Bishnoi dying had nothing to do with the drought. They had been beheaded in the year 1730 while trying to prevent outsiders from chopping down their green trees for firewood. Many other Bishnoi have died since then, attempting to stop poachers from killing wild game, or people taking plants from the region. Such martyrdom on behalf of other animals and plants is unprecedented, even in a society like India's that, in principle, reveres cows, and respects many other animals because of a widespread belief in reincarnation, as well as the legacy of ahimsa.

The government's award was part of its effort to educate the rural young and halt the mounting assault on the Indian environment. The award carried with it no financial assistance from the government. But, as I was to discover, beyond the smoking ruins of the dead cattle, the Bishnoi needed no money. They were the ones who were doing fine, who went about their business with a blessed impunity from famine and drought. How was it possible? Might their secrets, whatever they were, be applicable in Africa?

My wife Jane and I travelled over 2400 kilometres through the desert. I remember seeing the Bishnoi for the first time off in the hazy distance, stretching like a train of swaying jewels, hot dabs of colour beneath the long tedious ridge of dune. Lime green, magenta and blistering orange-draped women who balanced brass half-shells filled with dirt on top of their heads while men in white dhotis and shockingly white turbans dug into the sand. Fifty or so of them, in all, were working on one of many well-digging projects. I walked a kilometre over the white-caked plain to talk to them. I was greeted with affection. No water, they explained. They would dig three meters that day through the sand, before the overcrowded, diesel-spewing public carrier trucks would take them back to their village of Dechu. The next day they would return and dig for another twelve hours. The water table might be as deep as eighty meters, they explained.

Jane, with her long golden hair and brilliant blue eyes, showed up a few minutes later. This caused a sensation. Soon, it was decided that she was to be made an honorary "sister" of one of the young women in the tribe. Festooned in decorative gold jewelry beneath their glowing veils, the young women were fiercely curious. Other than their mild, almost whimsical manner of chastising the rainless sky, they did not seem like a community in trouble. Indeed, they were not, as we were soon to discover.

Meanwhile, the village elder reminisced about Mr. Eisenhower, whom he said he'd met in Panama during the Second World War. I informed him that Eisenhower had died many years before, and he expressed his surprise and his condolences with a show of remorse that was unusual. Then he returned to his shovel.

Later in the day, we visited a Bishnoi village. What we saw astonished us. Amid clusters of desert agony, here was an oasis of self-sustainability and serenity. Plants were green, gardens lush.

The Bishnoi's ardor to protect their environment, down to the least herb, dates from the 15th century. Jangeshwar Baghwan, or Jamboje, born in 1452 in the Rajasthani village of Pipasar, was elevated to the status of saint for the Bishnoi when he came forth with a series of revelatory decrees, each linked explicitly to ecology (an unnamed science as yet); and to the Bishnoi's spiritual approach to life. The Bishnoi believe him to be a descendant of Vishnu, the Hindu godhead. Jamboje's book of revelations, *Jamsagar* (loosely translated, the title means "show the people light"), describes a complex interrelationship of animals, plants and humans. And, for 500 years, the Bishnoi have followed his edicts as the basis of their faith: preserve the environment—that is the only spiritual and physical sustenance one requires.

We were led into the cellar darkness of a small temple built in memory of the Baghwan, and there, a copy of the *Jamsagar* was placed in my hands and some of its highlights read aloud to me, while dozens of villagers stood around us anxiously anticipating Jane's and my response.

Obedient to the edicts of the book, no Bishnoi will kill an animal or a tree. As strict vegetarians, they will not eat after dark to avoid the possibility of an insect getting into their food and being accidentally consumed. The

Bishnoi revere the khejare, *Prosopis cineraria*, a hearty thick-trunked tree that is native to northern Rajasthan. The Bishnoi prune it carefully to supply dried twigs from the upper part for fuel and building wood, and leaves to feed people and cattle. Jamboje recognized that cows love these leaves. Not surprisingly, researchers have since found that they contain a higher proportion of protein—11 to 14 per cent by weight—than any other leaf in the region. Cattle stay healthy fed on these leaves so Jamboje made the tree inviolate. Without the khejare tree, he said, there would be no cattle and thus no Bishnoi. Even as the famine persisted, the people took no more leaves than usual.

Jamboje also understood the dangers of uncontrolled grazing by livestock. Consequently, the Bishnoi have never reared sheep or goats, because of the effect these animals have on the land, reducing areas of grass and bush to desert. The Bishnoi breed their cattle selectively and match their food to their use. "Style-feeding" is a technique that the Bishnoi's neighbors in Rajasthan do not employ, and they should. The Bishnoi also monitor the foraging of their many camels very carefully, so that trees are cropped by the animals, but not damaged.

Bishnoi live in small communities, typically of about 100 families. They are settled pastoralists, and their food comes mainly from their livestock—milk, yoghurt and cheese. There are roughly four cattle to each person. The Bishnoi also grow food, which, like most desert people, they supplement with wild plants. Their houses are made of thatch woven from imported sugar cane stalks or bushy materials from the indigenous algoroba bean tree, *Prosopis juliflora*. Some villages use adobe to build houses. The Bishnoi dry dung for fuel; they do not use it to enrich their fields because they know that in the desert, dung—which is heavily acidic—can harm seedlings already overstressed.

In other words, the Bishnoi display a basic understanding of biology. Their spiritual identity is linked to the land and to its capacity—if nurtured—to support them. But unlike other environmentally sensitive tribal groups elsewhere in the world—the Bimin Kuskusmin of Papua, New Guinea, the Pygmies of Zaire, the Hadza of Tanzania, the Tasaday of Mindinao, and the Quolloyaha of northern Bolivia—the Bishnoi, like the urban Jains, are strict vegetarians.

While the Tar desert appears hostile, with temperatures that routinely exceed 110 degrees, the Bishnoi have learnt to extract every plant morsel of nourishment from the earth, without violating their reverance for life. Never in excess, never out of balance. In fact, Rajasthan's deserts are rich in nutrients if you have had the discipline and good sense to take note of the fact. Enormous cactus plants (*Euphorbia caducafolia*) turn golden at twilight while dozens of species of birds, including wild peacocks and eagles, literally walk across the pink desert floor. Rajasthani eagles saunter with the confidence of lions. Blackbucks, *chinkara* (small antelope), *nilgara* (large antelope known as blue bulls), wild dogs, jackals, desert fox and bobcat all live here. Like the antelope, the Bishnoi eat the hard-seeded berries and leaves of the *Ziziphus jujuba* bush, as well as the fruit of the *Capparis aphylla*, a medium-sized tree. They collect two endemic grass species, *Cynchrys ciliaris* and *bhaman*, which they feed to their mules and buffalos. Water gingerly harvested and collected in cisterns, then used for extremely concentrated (essentially drip) irrigation, enables the Bishnoi to grow two varieties of millet in summer, and radishes, carrots, garlic and onions in winter. They grow other crops as well, and trade dairy products in nearby towns for sesame oil, sorghum, wheat and at least four varieties of lentils, in addition to *lucerne* (alfalfa) for their cattle. These are the same foods that the Indian government had been shipping into the devastated (non-Bishnoi) Rajasthani communities at a rate of 200 truckloads a day to help to provide famine relief.

Jamboje evidently anticipated these droughts and famines. He said that one should expect such catastrophes every four years in the desert. I asked many of the Bishnoi about it and found that they were utterly unconcerned for themselves, though deeply saddened about the plight of their Rajput and Muslim neighbors. By tying their religion to ecology, they had managed to avoid the ravages of fluctuating meteorology and food supply. Research by the scientific advisers to the so-called Akhil Bhaitiya Jeev Raksha Bishnoi Sabha, the registered Indian society for environmental protection in the area, suggests that five years of drought had hardly altered the incidence of disease and mortality among the Bishnoi. Nor had any Bishnoi joined the mass exodus of other groups out of the desert into the cities.

But the Bishnoi do not have it made, or not entirely. India is losing 1.5 million hectares of forest each year. Soil erosion is severe. Between March and October, the Bishnoi can see the strong winds extending the surrounding sand dunes, covering their farm land and preventing seeds from germinating. The problem of desertification in Rajasthan is made worse, as in the African Sahel, by the uncontrolled collection of wood for fuel, and the voracious foraging by domestic sheep, goats and migratory camels. The Bishnoi have tried to talk sense into some of the other offending farmers and herders, but the results have not yet provided any measure of reversal.

Traditionally, the neighboring agricultural states of Madhya Pradesh, Gujarat and Haryana, provided Rajasthan with a rain umbrella that limited the spread of the desert, but as of 1988 this, too, had disappeared as drought afflicted most of the country. The Indian government was spending approximately 70 million rupees in 1988 to transport fodder and water to the hardest-hit areas north of Jodhpur and west of Bikaner. As Jane and I drove through these regions, wind carried the smoke from the pyres of corpses out along the horizon.

Meanwhile, 450 fodder depots and 76 cattle camps had been established in an effort to revive stray and starving animals. The whole scene of dust and devastation, of weakly lowing heifers and emaciated bulls, of bones and remnants, struck of the end of the world. "We are sentimental about our cows in this country," said G. C. Kanuga, director of the cattle camps. But among the Bishnoi, it was not merely sentiment that impelled them to exercise the wise husbandry of Jamboje. Their way of life, however compromised by one of the worst droughts in the world, remained viable. The

Bishnoi had sanctified their environment for centuries and were now reaping the profound benefits.

Contemplating these facts out in the heat of the desert was uplifting, even surrounded by death. It rekindled in me the firm belief that people can, if they are spiritually motivated, do anything. Even something practical, like surviving.

At Jodhpur University, Dr. Mohnot acknowledged that the Bishnoi are an extremely important model of ecological prudence that much of the world might well emulate. "Our films, books, lectures and endless symposia are useful up to a degree," he said. "But ultimately they miss the boat. They come from the city and rarely filter down to the villages in crisis. What we need to see happening is an ecological sensibility that begins at the village level. That is why the Bishnoi are so significant."

The government agrees. In the spirit of the first National Environment Memorial at the Bishnoi village of Khejare south of Jodhpur, it plans additional monuments in memory of many Bishnoi martyrs, historical wardens of the environment. The role model of the Bishnoi has inspired other more recent movements in India—like the Chipko tree-huggers in the Himalaya. And, the Bishnoi may prove to be a model for much of Indian society in other ways. Like the Jains, they acknowledge no caste system and provide equal employment for both sexes. In addition, they encourage birth control, contraception and full family planning.

With a little dot of henna dabbed on her forehead, for which she exchanged a silk scarf, and kohl-rimmed eyes, Jane had become Ermai's sister, while thirty other girls and older women surrounded the both of them in irrepressible jubilation. Suddenly, Ermai took Jane's hand and placed a two rupee note in it. It was a gift of extraordinary proportions, all things considered.

Later, passing by the circular mud houses of their village, which sat cozily on an earth that had baked for too long, windswept, dusty, the air thick with fatigue and haze, I had to admire the sheer beauty and tenacity of the Bishnoi whose adamant love of the Earth was everything to them. Whose pragmatic beliefs and deeply affecting strategies—common sense and religion—had been passed down from generation to generation. How rare to encounter a spiritual exercise, if you like, that actually promoted the health of the planet; whose adherents were numerous; whose men and women and children prepared to sacrifice their lives on behalf of even a small shrub. A philosophy, borne of meditation, released into the world in the form of praxis.

The Bishnoi would survive as long as their love survived. Jane and I were dazed by the depth of feelings we had experienced, their openness, generosity of spirit, and wisdom. I could imagine no more perfect form of community: vegetarian, self-sustainable, a balanced population, deep ecological sensibility that every child could work towards without fear of metaphysical ambiguity.

As we left the Bishnoi paradise, the desert itself looked different than ever before. No longer was the scoured bedrock a harbinger of despair; nor did gutted alkaline flats, emergency convoys, and the funeral pyres of dead camel and buffalo engender hopelessness. The desert would bloom again. The Bishnoi knew how to make it happen.[2]

[1]*The Life of Marpa the Translator*, p. 188, Tsang Nyon Heruka, Prajna Press, 1982.
[2]This essay has been adapted from the author's article, "Desert Survival by the Book," published in the *New Scientist*, December 17, 1988, Vol. 120, No. 1643,

VII
A Paradox of Souls

In this city of corpses I sing of God's goodness,
and I strike this note of warning…

—Guru Nanak[1]

Most ecologists rightly claim that human overpopulation is the planet's number one dilemma, a crisis mired by political, economic, cultural and spiritual uncertainty. All other ecological woes result from the greatly excessive numbers of one species. Yet overpopulation is not defined by its density or number, but by its impact. And this means that Americans, Japanese and Western Europeans are the most over-populated of all cultures. The solution to that must come from within individuals who consciously set out to diminish their own personal impact. Once again, meditation can lead to action.

How can one think about overpopulation without falling prey to a useless lip service that has no relevance to anyone? No issue causes more cross-cultural rancor, cries of racism, sexism, colonialism, imperialism, and—most of all—an overwhelming pessimism, than that of overpopulation. The miracle of people, the trauma of our numbers, is the door handle of evolution. Close the door or open the door. What will it be? What are the ramifications? The next da Vinci, or the next Stalin? Of self-consciousness and restraint, or of slovenly evil? A gift without limitation or a gift to be nurtured cautiously? The divine pleasures of infinity or the lessons of a finite world, with its runaway consumption, cultural entrapment, political powerlessness and devastating ecological impact?

Both the da Vincis and the Stalins, and everyone else, are by-products of hormones, fantasies, love, or ignorance; ignorance in the sense that this century's riot of *Homo sapiens* is spinning exponentially out of control, nearly quadrupling itself. The most terrifying analogy I have heard is that of the eutrophic lake. Its biological oxygen demand and its fungal infestations double every day. One morning, on the 29th day, the lake is half covered with algal slime. That leaves half a lake to drink and enjoy and not worry about. In twenty four hours however—one more doubling time— the entire lake is unexpectedly dead, a seething swamp. In fact, there is nothing unexpected about it. It's only a question of when the human population reaches its 29th day.

What can any individual do to avoid the stupidity of perpetuating excess? How could any introversion produce the seed of a called-for turn-around? The stubborn seeds of overpopulation are rooted to several million years of hominid sexuality, as well as to the more recent stupefying pervasiveness of most forms of pride, insecurity, poverty and the various cultures' evangelical edicts.

The answer is obvious enough: to all future couples; to those who would have children, reproduce only once. Beyond that, adopt existing foundlings and set an example to your children of minimal consumption and non-violence, which obviously includes total vegetarianism. These injunctions are simple. At least, on paper.

In most of Europe, North America, and Japan, zero population growth (ZPG) has indeed become a virtual reality, though at least two more generations will be born before the fertility momentum truly stops. This slowing down has been celebrated by Western government agencies and most environmentalists. But there is a fatal flaw to that euphoria: in truth, the ZPG countries are the most grossly overpopulated nations in the history of the human race and procreative restraint will not alter that fact, either presently or in the future. This trend towards ZPG is not resulting in less consumption, less waste, decreased environmental degradation, or fewer animals slaughtered—though in theory it should. Our individual footprints, already the size of dinosaurs', are still getting larger, our claws sharper, the potency of our population size ever more injurious. This paradox is called by population theorists, "The Netherlands Fallacy."

A newborn American will consume between 200 and 400 times his counterpart in most impoverished countries. This equivalency is derived from statistics at the grocery and department stores, from utility companies and homeowner's associations, from Wall Street, police, airline and annual car manufacturing reports; from the veterinarians and hospitals and chemical companies and feedlots; the agricultural conglomerates, the Departments of State, Commerce, Interior, Agriculture, from the Pentagon, the banks, and the Environmental Protection Agency. The statistics come from everywhere—from courthouses in Europe where litigation is in progress over American toxic dumping on NATO bases; from West Africa where we have shipped our dioxin; from Indonesia where we have arrogantly sold DDT, knowing full well that it is noxious. And from India, where our government has deliberately pawned off its outdated surplus environmental control technologies, when other, Best Available Technology should have been discounted, to help ease the servicing of external debt in India,

Brazil, Mexico or Kenya, thereby encouraging environmental self-sustainability. These are pieces of the puzzle of our global impact, the result of overpopulation at home.

But the real derivation of such statistics is not in the international believing, but the local seeing. And the sight is one too easily recognizable by most urban or suburban Americans. Just look outside. Listen to the air. Put your fingers to your temples.

The American child is not one person, but as many as 400 persons, consuming, killing, laying waste. He may not be a da Vinci or a Stalin but, at the very least, he is a giant, inadvertently incurring the perpetuation of a self-destructive system. The arithmatic requires no special pedigree of logic, but should be self-evident: 250 million Americans times 400, which translates into an ecological impact the equivalent of 100 billion people. My thinking grapples for the best way to symbolize that obesity: 1.2 billion people in China, 900 million people in India, 100 billion in the U.S. Less than 500 million in all of Africa, but 100 billion in the U.S.

There are other ways, beyond the sheer avalanche of stellar numbers to recall the significance of our overpopulation. Its truth hinges upon the essential definition of the phrase, which is the ability of an ecosystem to safely absorb numbers of any given species.

Environmental carrying capacity need not have anything to do with density. Africa is not densely populated. Nor was Sukwutnu, the Yokut Indian name for their city which once existed beside a now dried-up inland lake between Fresno and Bakersfield. Sukwutnu was home to over 20,000 Native Americans, whose diet was essentially vegetarian. They lived in yurts, carried on trade with Indians in the High Sierra, and for centuries defied the modern urban planner's assumption that a city means environmental destruction; that it is not possible for a so-called metropolitan statistical region to tread lightly on its surroundings. But that's exactly what these dense congeries of Yokut were able to accomplish, and it was a triumph worthy of intense adulation. Unhappily, they—like most Native Americans—lost that light touch upon life when their own lives were invaded by unthinking, uncaring, violent outsiders: Spanish, Portuguese, Christian missionaries, American settlers and soldiers. Vegetarians turned into meat-eaters and desperados, a word coined almost precisely to fit their hopeless circumstance.

The message of Sukwutnu is a hopeful one, however. It is possible to generate a large community that is sustainable. But the urgent message of Sukwutnu is hardly perceivable beneath the onorous veil of a domestic invasion still very much in vogue, as witnessed by the damage done to the San Joaquin valley, where the Yokut once lived. California's agricultural belt is drying up, the hundreds of chemicals leaching into the ground water, poisoning the soil, stripping it of its nutrients. Ground water is being sucked up for the cities, and places like the shrinking Mono Lake are the result. At the Salton Sea, hundreds of thousands of birds, mostly the beautiful grebes, have died from toxic agricultural run-off. All outcomes of an overpopulated

California which never once stopped to examine the agricultural techniques of the natives that farmed the land in harmony with nature.

The Native Americans were the canaries, the barometric reading; their plight at the hands of the outsiders was evidence of the ferocity of the storm, the poisons in the mine shaft. Then it was the forests, of which 75 percent have been chopped down; the bison, once numbering eighty million, now reduced to a few thousand. The litany of destruction quickly escalated. In California, the Yokuts essentially disappeared by 1850. Along with the Native Americans, most of California's wildlife died out.

But the killing continues. The eruptions of violence in South Central Los Angeles, and in Santa Monica and Beverly Hills, and nearly every other quadrant of the 4000-square-mile L.A. County, merely highlight the ongoing scenario of daily murders in that unintelligble expanse of a city. The personal anxiety which can so easily invoke a violent reaction follows the same behavioral predictability and rules of entropy that apply to any other animal species trapped in a labyrinth, physically denied the basics of life: clean water, clean air, a food supply, darkness at night, plentiful rest, limited noise, loving companions, a sense of security, in short, a relatively stress-free environment. The California Condor, the El Segundo Blue Butterfly, the Yokut, like the rest of us, are all victims of the same tragic syndrome. Here in California, to paraphrase Governor Cuomo, children grow up hearing gunblasts long before they've ever heard a symphony.

Every creek is polluted, the aquifers are drying up, the variety of our crop species dwindling as corporate monoculture—with its arsenal of life-threatening chemicals—replaces nearly all family farming in California. The air is foul (though the California weather, which, of course, is remarkably mild, easily masks that fact), the garbage piling up, the crisis of the homeless, of abused women and children, escalating. The entire system—from the freeways to the courts—is overloaded.

For all of its exotic botanical imports, its grassy knolls north of San Vicente Boulevard, and hillside estates above Sunset, Los Angeles is more inorganic than organic now, a miasma of concrete, glass, tarmac. Every year in the county, several thousand people die as a direct or indirect result of environmental pollution. The state health department does not require autopsies in cases of suspected pollution poisoning, and so epidemiologists must contend with guesswork and the most likely cause of death, in cases of emphysema and other acute respiratory and cardiac problems exacerbated by those days deemed "Stage 1," or "Stage 2" smog alert.

Los Angeles is overpopulated. When even its predators are dying out—mountain lions, coyotes, the condor—a city, any city, should recognize a problem. The fact that California's official mascot, the grizzly bear, disappeared entirely from California back around the time of the Depression, is ample evidence that man has overstepped his place in the kingdom.

In South Florida, the same levels of impact are attributable to too many souls. South Florida has been compared in population density and increase to Bangladesh. Hurricane and tidal disasters have strikingly analogous impacts on the two regions. The state has a 2.8 percent per year population increase (versus a 0.7 increase in most of America). There are nearly 14 million people residing there currently, many additional part-timers (people with second homes and condos near the beaches). 25 percent of the population are elderly immigrants from elsewhere, many retired, living off Social Security and quickly falling behind inflation. Some are malnourished. Those 14 million have virtually killed off most of the once abundant manatees, cougars and rich bird life. From Lake Okeechobee to the Everglades and Florida Bay and the Keys, the state—like the rest of the country, the rest of the world—has witnessed an ecological collapse that coincides with the American Dream.

Miami, like Tokyo, Manhattan, Frankfurt, London, and Amsterdam—like all the other bloated conurbations in the developing world, is overpopulated—not just cities like Calcutta and Sao Paolo.

In the Netherlands, where this fallacy of behavior has achieved its most paradoxical zenith, the earthworms are dying out from chemical pollution. And while Amsterdam's canals invite the meditation of tourists and painters, and the riot of tulips is everywhere commended, the country as a whole is utterly dependent on the importation of its grain, energy and the majority of its foodstuffs. The Netherlands cultivated a taste for all things foreign during its Golden Age of mercantilism. Back then, spices, gold filigree, exotic woods and Oriental imports accounted for the bulk of shipped goods to Rotterdam. Today, Holland's very life hangs in the balance of packing slips, ledgers and foreign accounts. What this means, ecologically speaking, is that the country—with a density of population exceeding 1000 per square mile—is utterly out-of-touch with its own domestic nature.

Is this equally true in Bangladesh, a country which has come to symbolize to Westerners oblivious to their own expansive numbers at home,¡¡ the very quintessence of overpopulation and hopelessness? In the winter of 1975, during one of the worst famines in that country, I worked handing out bags of powdered milk at a refugee camp outside of Dacca, where some 50,000 individuals sat or lay in the dirt, holding their heads, their stomachs, crying, groaning, or too sick and exhausted to make a sound. They were starving to death and a little powdered milk for the day, along with a biscuit, was certainly not going to save them. I knew it, they knew it. At that time Bangladesh had something like 88 million residents. Today, 112 million.

But what was true then, even in the midst of famine, is true today: the country is lush and has sufficient arable land to produce more than enough food for its population. That will change, of course, with time, as Western nations sell higher and higher technology to the Bengalis and their own poverty begins to change toward riches. But the irony is inherent, here. As the riches escalate, the arable land will diminish. The population momentum will continue for many decades, one disaster cascading after another.

But, for now, the famine in a land of plenty invites other more immediate contradictions which countless organizations have pointed out, drawing the attention of lending banks and policy planners to the real source of hunger, namely, poor transportation systems, insufficient funds to buy food, and the conversion of prime agricultural lands to cash crop farms which manage to reduce a country's debt burden but do nothing to feed local people who are starving. Famine has little to do with the diminishing size of family holdings, or the landless. In most of the world, a farm means a small garden plot, which is usually sufficient to raise enough food for a family, unless that family has ten people, not uncommon; or that garden is given over not to vegetables, but rather, to jute or cotton which may generate a few dollars of currency that can in turn be used to pay off debts or to buy cooking fuel.

Famine and overpopulation suggest yet a second sphere of contradiction. To many, the logic of infant mortality should hold that the more babies that die, the less severe the crisis of overpopulation. The same can be said for AIDS, malaria, chronic dysentery, plagues and war, or, for that matter, famine. Most deaths from hunger are not famine-related, but long-term in nature. People, mostly children, suffer every moment, year after year, until they die, unknown, uncared for, often not even buried. Who are these people that we are so eager to write off? Whose plight, we would like to imagine, is self-neutralizing in biological terms?

There were many in Bangladesh who offered me food though they were themselves hungry; who smiled courageously, though they were dying. This is more than mere humanity: this is a miracle. And it must penetrate our consciousness to the marrow. The preciousness of every child summons the courage to help them live. In the last twenty-five years, 200 million children have died needlessly. By the planet's own reckonings and numeric balancing act, perhaps those deaths were essential. Locusts and lemmings, lynxes and hares appear to abide by boom-and-bust mathematics which keep their numbers in check.

In Zimbabwe, a country that has made remarkable strides in family planning (over 30 percent of the women now use birth control, ten times the average throughout the rest of Africa), they are in deep trouble with AIDS. Twenty percent of the country is now infected, 90 percent of the work force may be dying within a decade.

Does that mean that efforts to curtail overpopulation and hunger are all for naught? By humanity's standards, in my humble opinion, any effort to foster love and care is crucial to what we are about. Lose that characteristic and we are lost.

So what is the answer? And how can one person's thinking make a difference? Clearly Albert Gore's own resonant contemplation of the issues, his well-informed stance, helped win his place on the 1992 Democratic ticket. Gore, in his book, *Earth In The Balance*, writes compassionately and knowingly of overpopulation. Individuals—be they a Schweitzer or a Gorbachev—make the difference. And while it may be a cliché, there is at least small comfort in the abiding truth of it, as in the hope that global policy changes can, and will be enacted through the increasing influence of such people.

What kind of policy changes?

According to the World Health Organization, every day people make love approximately 100 million times, with a resulting one million conceptions and 150,000 abortions. For the amount of love being sustained, that's less then a one percent population increase at best. It does not exactly correspond with other statistics which show the world's population adding nearly 100 million new souls every year—17 million in Africa, 55 million in Asia, 10 million in Latin America. Our species is rapidly increasing towards a presumed levelling off at somewhere between ten and fifteen billion human beings by the middle of the next century. But that is a figure which does not take into account western style consumers and their impact, their numbers stretching towards the equivalent of half-a-trillion people on the planet.

In countries like Mali, Brazil, Mexico, Burkina Faso, Nigeria (expected to reach half-a-billion by the year 2050), Ethiopia and Somalia, Kenya (the world's champion in population growth with eight children per family and a growth rate of 4.3 percent per year, a doubling of the nation's total population every 24 years), Saudi Arabia, Egypt, the Philippines, Indonesia (the island of Java alone contains 120 million people), Bangladesh, China and India, there seems at first glance to be little hope that human restraint and governmental wisdom can stave off total disaster.

Saudi Arabia, one of the richest countries in the world, has not been inclined to restrain its numbers, which academic theory suggests is always a correlary of wealth. The Saudis, like most of the Arab world, have between six and seven children per woman. The *Koran* does not oppose abortion, but the marked inferior status of women in Moslem countries has made them sex slaves, furnishing its own population bomb. There are currently some one billion Moslems in the world.

China indeed succeeded in cutting its fertility rate by half, an unprecedented achievement. But China's 1.2 billion people will add yet 400 million more before ZPG, and that 1.6 billion has grand ideas about resource extraction and consumerism. They have only begun to buy, to dig, to burn, to drink. If they should prosper and attain even a partial degree of what Hong Kong has done for itself, the numbers game and its equivalency in terms of overall ecological impact will be on an order of magnitude that even dwarfs America and Japan.

That scenario is even more terrifying in India. There, the nature of the soul (*Atman*, or *Jiva*) has been described and belabored for a least 4000 years. Pan-Indian culture was the first to advance the notion of a universal soul, of an I-Thou relationship between an individual and all of creation. In the quest after a spiritual life, various stages of experience (spiritual evolution) were prescribed in the diverse body of religious literature—whether Jain, Hindu, Buddhist or Islamic. And the central core of that experience always recommended family and lots of children. India is currently adding sixteen million newborns every year, while 4000 children die there every day of hunger. There are nearly 900 million Indians, currently. The country's ability to expand agriculturally is severely limited. Food production levels are declining. Despite it being the first nation to utilize family planning policy, India is looking at two billion people by 2050, more souls than inhabited the entire planet in the early 20th century. At the same time, the country is rapidly industrializing, its cities adding millions every year to the ranks of the homeless, its environment reeling under the load of pollutants, deforestation, soil erosion, salinization, desertification and the rapid loss of biodiversity.

What does this all mean? Is ancient, spiritual India is on the brink of…what, collapse? Explosion? Another Haiti?

Haiti has one of the most quickly deteriorating ecological scenarios in the world, having lost more than 50 percent of its food self-sufficiency since 1968. Meanwhile, its population percentage increase is equivalent to that of India. But, unlike India, or China, or any of the African nations, Haiti has no more space to expand. The island, with its murderous dictatorship and absence of most human rights, is the world's premiere environmental basket case. Haiti's crisis has become America's own crisis. The land once proud of its hospitality, the myth that once propagated the words, "Give me your huddled masses…," now turns its back.

I don't know the words. Collapse…Explosion…Haiti….I do know that 80 percent of the world's poor, or 4 billion, are to be found in developing countries. The majority of these people are young, under fifteen, and suffering. Families on average contain nearly five children and half of them are living in over-crowded cities.

Mexico City is destined to reach a population of nearly thirty million fairly soon. There are two million Mexican newborns each year, and some of them—the *pepenadores*—end up scavenging through garbage dumps for their food, like those of the Netzahualcoyotl slum on the edge of the capital. With its 100 billion dollar debt and mounting pollution, the country needs help. America is her neighbor. America needs to be neighborly and the recent economic pact that would open up the border between the two countries has been viewed in that spirit.

But neighbors can only do so much, especially when they have their own mounting crises at home. And with Mexico's less evolved state of environmental protection, the economic boom which the recent pact promises is likely to further increase the burden of ecological decay afflicting both sides of the border.

Only the forces of nature will determine the fate of the existing billions of excess people. But the future need not be left so up to chance. What the world needs is a comprehensive global strategy, a united front that advocates and gently but forcefully persuades men and women to have no more than one child per couple. I said it earlier, but it is worth repeating: curbing overpopulation is mankind's only hope of reclaiming the balance which can ensure ecological stability on Earth. Is that wishful thinking? Probably, if one were to speak with the Pope or the Republican Party, at present, or with your average Haitian or Indian or Muslim. But in the depths of my heart, where conflict has subsided and the inner workings of every day seek solace in something beyond the vagaries of numbers and flow charts and the politics of despair, there are five reasons to be hopeful.

Five Reasons for Hope

First: We have the technical know-how to change our past methods. As suspicious as I am of "solutions," which often come masked as gift-horses or opiates, nevertheless I have seen real possibilities for redemption among Jains, Bishnoi and sensitive people throughout the world.

In the case of overpopulation and famine, those possibilities cry out all around us. As far back as 1979, the National Academy of Sciences and the National Research Council, as reported by the late Robert Rodale, recommended some startling and well-tested "anti-famine" plants that could, without much difficulty, end hunger on this earth. They included such crops as the African yam bean, the Bambara groundnut, the desert date and hausa potato, tamarind and amaranth and nearly 2000 others. Rodale's Institute in Pennsylvania has spent millions of dollars to advance a technique known by scientists and farmers as alley cropping, a method of separating out different indigenous species from one another by planting them between rows of drought resistant shade trees and bushes like Leucaena, or the desert *Prosopis cineraria* (the Omani Tree of Life, of the same genus as is found in Bishnoi country), or the Gliricidia hedgerow.

In addition, a greater emphasis on the use of innovative water catchment techniques to harvest the most meager precipitation would mean more cisterns in desert areas. Nearly 1750 edible plant species of the Halophyte family that tolerate brackish, saline water have been identified, species that are applicable to much of the world and hold the potential for holding back the desert, generating wood for fuel and shade, and food for hungry people. With 26 billion fewer tons of topsoil available every year because of human neglect, such natural food possibilities are urgently needed. The solutions are before us.

Second: Family planning has now reached nearly every country in the world. In some places, like China, Tunisia and Zimbabwe, the results have been dramatic. Women in developing countries had, on average, just under four children in the period 1985-1990, compared with more than six children in the period 1965-1970. In the United States, with Democratic sensibility coming back into power, the unbelievable damage done by twelve years of conservative Republican politics may be reversed and ecological common sense once again made to work in the world. Like the Vatican, the Reagan/ Bush administrations attempted to renounce overpopulation as an issue. But, unlike the Vatican, whose policies are perceived by most of the world's 900 million Roman Catholics—especially in Italy—to be counter-productive, the Republican Party has managed to shape its extremism into law, extending its backward arm to the Supreme Court, making the female body and its priorities a matter for jurists to decide, and cutting off international family planning funds, because they assumed that complicity with family planning meant the condoning of abortion. But with a new era of sound environmental policy, that primeval thinking will be forever silenced. Drugs like RU486 will be re-introduced into the United States, and our encouragement of birth control elsewhere in the world enhanced through financial assistance. But once again, such hopes will only be realized if individuals figure it out for themselves and make their beliefs known.

Third: Relating to family planning and to individuals, sexual partners using any kind of contraception in Third World countries between 1960 and 1965 numbered but 31 million. Today, the numbers approach 400 million. With the tragic onset of AIDS, the awareness of the need for contraception has certainly spread and will continue to do so.

Fourth: The awareness of overpopulation and of ecological impact in general, was sorely lacking from the world's consciousness even as late as 1970. Today, as Senator Gore put it so succinctly in his speech at the Democratic Convention, in the post-Cold War era, safeguarding the environment must be the central core of any political philosophy and practice. Problems cannot be solved until they are understood. And, while we have not yet imagined the scope of humankind's damage to the planet, we know that it is enormous; that it is 100 percent our fault, and that we've got to do something about it, now. Our understanding is evolving rapidly.

Fifth: That nascent understanding has already signalled a coming revolution in deep ecological ethics, in alternative energy usage, in decontamination and bio-remediation techniques, and in community and individual empowerment. This latter effect was most evident at the Rio Summit, where the real talent and ideas and energy were not to be found among governments and their representatives, but in the thousands of people there on behalf of the various NGOs, or non-governmental organizations, such as the Unao de Vegetal of Brazil, a group committed to promoting sustainable practices in the Amazon. Even in Bangladesh, there are an estimated 3000 non-governmental organizations currently working to solve the overpopulation and hunger crises in that country. In Mali, one of the hungriest places on earth, there are innovative new women's farming collectives and solar power installations. Has hunger been solved there? Not yet, but give it time. In India and Sri Lanka, the Sarvodaya Shramadana movement, founded by A. T. Ariyaratne, now has more than 30,000 grassroots organizers in villages across the sub-continent working in areas of family planning and sustainability. The ten largest banks in the world, all in Japan, along with the World Bank and International Monetary Fund, have a new role to play in the facilitation of these NGOs' goals.

I think back to my first day at Tongee, in Bangladesh, and the sight of that abominable grief and hopelessness that had gripped the dying. That had transformed the breasts of young mothers into milkless dried-out sacks, sallow and shrunken and looking 100 years old. It was a vision of death and disease and pain, all of them unnecessary.

The technical, political and moral solutions are there to be initiated. All that is required are the individuals to make them happen. Those who are not hungry, who have power, are the ones who have to help. Responsibility becomes them. Awareness becomes everyone. But beyond awareness, as Nikos Kazantzakis put it, "The ultimate, most holy form of theory is action."[2]

[1]Guru Nanak, early 16th century, in *The Heritage of the Sikhs*, by Harbans Singh, p. 22, Asia Publishing House, New York, N.Y.
[2]Nikos Kazantzakis, *The Saviors of God—Spiritual Exercises*, p. 99. Translated by Kimon Friar, Simon & Schuster, New York, 1960.

VIII
What is Human?

Let us be humane to each other, and the spirit of humanity will naturally extend itself to the whole kinship of life.

—George William Foote

In this meditation, I suggest that our physical evolution was completed tens of thousands of years ago. Since at least the Upper Paleolithic, human speciation has been occurring mentally. Our inner thoughts have driven our evolution and will continue to do so. The ramifications of this are spectacular.

One of the most insistent challenges to human reason is its unreason; the massacres waged throughout time, the evil which persists in the minds of certain men. How is it possible that the same species can harbor an Albert Schweitzer and an Adolf Hitler?

There seems little hope of ever illuminating this paradox by reference to biology. It is enough to acknowledge that the human species, having comprised something like 100 billion individuals in the last 50,000 years, enjoys a wide enough variability in its races and attitudes to host every conceivable point of view, artistic grace and insanity. But whether the world is large enough for every opinion, or for each of us to be wrong, is doubtful. The world is not large enough, not by any recent ecological yardsticks.

The genetics of personality are a vastly imperfect science. Organic diseases are traceable, at times, to quirks in the chemistry, some inheritable, others not. But there is no accounting, as they say, for taste. Furthermore, the nature/nurture debate sheds less and less light on this matter as the environment in which children are raised becomes increasingly fragmented.

There is no longer a reliable compass reading on what it is that truly constitutes *Homo sapiens*. If one were discussing, say, *Polistes gallicus*, the

French wasp which builds a complicated nest much like an apartment building, or *Triticum durum*, hard wheat, or *Loxodonta africana*, the African elephant, or even *Canis familiaris*, the family dog, there would be a much greater level of confidence for ascribing traits, even a certain destiny to those organisms. But human beings—whom Aristotle described as *Zoon politikon*, the "political animal"—are not predictable.[2] There is no certainty about them, nothing that can be said with confidence, other than that they eat, they sleep, they eliminate their waste, they procreate, they die.

That political animal might point to valid grounds for asserting that Schweitzer and Hitler were both attempting to do good, as ghastly as the juxtaposition sounds. "To see a good in evil, and a hope in ill-success," wrote Robert Browning ("Paracelsus," iv.) "I form the light and create darkness. I make peace, and create evil. I, the Lord, do all these things," said Isaiah (xiv. 7). "I am generation and dissolution...I am sunshine and I am rain...I am death and immortality. I am entity (reality) and non-entity (non-reality)," related Shri Krishna in the *Bhagavad Gita*.

A tyrant, like the healer, had a vision of nobility, of purity and health. A madman considered himself sane, while a sane man thought the world filled with pain and insanity. Both strove to eradicate cancers, goiters and anomalies. One called them Jews, the other thought of them in more normal medical terms.

Inhumanity has no place in this argument, if a species is considered a species. Most people are not busy systematically executing millions of others, though most of us are not hurrying to volunteer with U.N. ground forces in Bosnia, or Cambodia, or infiltrating slaughterhouses in order to sabotage the genocide taking place there. According to the argument of means, whatever is in Hitler must be in Schweitzer, and vice versa; that our biology must unify us, however variable those thought processes which commandeer the whims and dreams and methods of individuals.

But there is something altogether sinister about this theory of unity, not just because it encourages the strict logician to play devil's advocate and merge the monstrous with the saintly. Nor simply because it tends to dismiss those individual differences which so account for the magnificence of human beings, our biological monotony aside. But because it focuses on biology itself, the brute mechanism, whose evolutionary impetus amounts to all of a few hundred bones and muscles that are going nowhere new; an organism that more or less achieved its current physical status tens of thousands of years ago.

What has happened, largely as a result of the advent of fire[3], is the rapid and continuing expansion of the neo-cortex, of thought. And not just any thought, but introspective hours, millennia after millennia; the kind of thinking which, characteristically, takes on the philosophical breadth of a campfire; what millions of dreams are made of. Such thinking, from the time of *Homo erectus*, has been tantamount to human evolution. Biologically one would speak in terms of brain growth during gestation, as compared with earlier primate fetal life. The *Homo erectus* fetus acquired 20,000 neurons a minute. During the third trimester, its brain accumulated 2.2 milligrams a minute, weighing 382 grams at birth.[4]

For *Homo sapiens* ("wise man"), the growth curves are even more dramatic. What this all suggests is that biological evolution was replaced, at some point, by the evolution of thought; that the human species refers to a vast menagerie of ideas which had long ago transcended the mere facts of a bipedal skeleton and consanguine ties.

To take this one step further, the crucial step, this new conceptual evolution implies that the word "species" is no longer uniformly applicable to human beings, or not as a single classifying agent. There must be more than one human species.

How is that so?

Because the principles upon which any species is thus named are strictly morphological, applying to conditions that have satisfied our rage for order in the plant and animal kingdom, but which tell us nothing about the actual evolutionary patterns among humans; neither the possibilities for future change, nor the spectacular growth and divergences of thought by which we must be fundamentally characterized.

The notion of species is a system of barricades that has simply fortified mankind's arrogance and isolationism against his better instincts. These divisions, codified by science and absolutist in the force of their subtle acceptance by most people, are contrary to the innocent longings and affection for the whole world which are exhibited in nearly every child, whose vision is pantheistic, all-embracing; afraid, in truth, of neither ghosts nor goblins; neither lions nor tigers nor bears. In Biblical times, Adam and Eve named the animals not from any scientific questing after truth, but—as Mark Twain imagined in his *Diaries* of the original couple—for the sheer delight in invention. But this arbitrary name-calling has resulted in a comprehensive intransigence, in steadfast blinders that have cut us off, surrounded us by strangers that roar in the night. Biologically autistic, we languish on an artificial island of our own making, narcissistic, unconnected. One would think that people everywhere would have become quite close, as ones who have ghettoized themselves within the animal kingdom. Ironically, that is anything but the case.

It was the Swedish taxonomist Carolus Linnaeus (1707-1778) who first conceived of a binomial nomenclature that divided the organic world into Kingdom, Phylum, Class, Order, Family, Genus, Species, Sub-species and Variations. But what was the actual basis for this obsession with categories and differences? Biological structure in plants, not complex thinking in man. From his first appointment as a lecturer in botany, to his later botanical explorations throughout Lapland, Linnaeus' passion had to do with stamens and pistils. His major works, *Systema Naturae, Species Plantarum, Genera Plantarum* and *Hortus Cliffortianus*, were premised upon the variability and reproductive strategies of plants, principally. And this system of expediency has been adhered to ever since, even though it seems to have little relevance to human beings or other animals.

A species is traditionally defined as any group of organisms who are able to reproduce among themselves, but cannot do so with other groups of organisms. This insular credo of fertility has become the measure of every biological barrier and every ego in the world. We have supported our own colossal hubris by this ingenius little word, "species," by which we mean to establish the prestige of ourselves and the hierarchy of men in a world of allegedly lesser beings. Our homocentric presumption of unity has granted us the right to demean and demolish all other life forms as we see fit.

Yet a close reading of Charles Darwin yields a somewhat modified set of generalizations, not so readily given to this amateurish penchant for unity and simple classification in a world of complexity.

Darwin's first edition of *The Origin of Species* on November 24, 1859, followed in the wake of dozens of other zoologists and philosophers who had publicly speculated on the nature of evolution and genetic descent, largely as a result of the British mania for hybridizing plants and the practical wisdom gained as a result. It was Darwin and Alfred Wallace who applied these same cross-breeding verities to certain odd characteristics which they had noted among animals, especially birds. The idea of evolution, of descent from a common ancestor, in contrast with the much prevailing notion of each individual species having been "created" individually and separate and simultaneously, hinged upon the notion of relationships in nature, of *genera*. In his day, many of Darwin's fellow naturalists were only too eager to proliferate the number of species and genera in the world. But only to emphasize the prodigiousness of God's creation. Even the slightest variations, for example, among certain Brachiopod shells, or plants like Hieracium and Rubus, often prompted whole new classifications. Species were running riot on Earth, it was claimed.

Darwin was keen to uphold the fact of biodiversity, but was far less inclined to be so carefree in his appellations. He would write, "How many of the birds and insects in North America and Europe, which differ very slightly from each other, have been ranked by one eminent naturalist as undoubted species, and by another as varieties, or, as they are often called, geographical races!...Even Ireland has a few animals, now generally regarded as varieties, but which have been ranked as species by some zoologists....There is no possible test but individual opinion to determine which of them shall be considered as species and which as varieties...A wide distance between the homes of two doubtful forms leads many naturalists to rank them as distinct species..."[5]

And this same confusion, according to Darwin, engulfed Linnaeus' broader classifications, such that even families and genera were subject to nearly arbitrary attribution with respect to their comparative value.

One Genus, however, remained solitary, with only one species associated with it, namely, *Homo* and *Homo sapiens*.

And while anthropologists, philosophers and theologians might refer to the varieties of religious experience, or to the different races, physical types, histories, languages, customs, and myriads of attitudes and opinions that marked every individual, the scientific community never went so far as to claim multiple species within the *Homo* genus. Nevertheless, Darwin was indeed troubled by what he called "protean" or "polymorphic" variants. And he acknowledged that these morphological anomalies were found among men. "These individual differences are of the highest importance for us, for they are often inherited, as must be familiar to every one," he wrote.[6] He even went so far as to call these differences "incipient species," the likely result of a dominant species that was well diffused and had produced offspring of well-marked varieties.[7] As for ranking them as varieties, rather than as species, Darwin stated emphatically that the "amount of difference considered necessary to give to any two forms the rank of species cannot be defined."[8]

In some instances, Darwin ascribed more certainty to the distinction of lesser organisms. He cites such defining physiological characteristics as the inner passage between nostril and mouth in reptiles and fishes, the articulation of the lower jaw in Marsupials, the way in which certain insects fold their wings, the color of Algae, the type of dermal covering in Vertebrata,[9] as clear examples of speciation.

These are the very forms and functions exploited by natural selection in its continuous quest for new adaptive strategies. And curiously, whether form follows function, or vice versa, has no bearing on the quality of mind, what the Jains call *jiva*, or soul; what Teilhard De Chardin named the *Zoosphere*; and what the early Roman philosopher Plotinus, referred to as *Nous*, the Universal Soul-Mind.

Human beings are not merely lower jaws or colors or dermal coverings. All of the physiological elements which comprise this species of ours may be enough to warrant a universal definition, but cannot come to actually distinguishing one man from another.

Beyond our looks or lung size, what is significant is our thought, whose diversity—over five billion current opinions about everything—constitutes fertile ground for assessing the evolution of new species, species of thought. These are, by their very nature, that which propagate, house, clothe, feed, fuel and involve all of us, but which conceptually ascend well beyond the mere pragmatics of sustenance. Thought which is both form and function, music and creator, chicken and egg. Thought which is passed down from generation to generation as sure as the proboscis of a feral pig, but which is subject to overnight elaboration like no physical property can be. Thought which carries in its neural web certain rudimentary attitudes that go beyond mere expediency or changeable opinion.

This is not an easy premise, particularly given the fact it dispenses with the genetic model of inheritance. Because there is no question that people are born neither good nor bad. Genetic disposition, even in the worst cases of congenital abnormality, are subject to amelioration in mind. Ideas engender realities. And ideas are free, contained by no prison, no body, no obligation. A person can change his or her attitude. No "bad seed" is necessarily permanent. Bertrand Russell once remarked that a true philosopher changes his mind every week. We're all students of experience.

And yet, statistically, there are at least two clear invariants in human conceptual evolution, namely, good and evil. They may be mixed up in some people, but they operate nevertheless.

Freud considered aggression and resulting evil as part of our instinctual endowment, as much as laughter and nurturance. As paleontologist Raymond Dart wrote, "The blood-bespattered, slaughter-gutted archives of human history from the earliest Egyptian and Sumerian records to the most recent atrocities of the Second World War accord with early universal cannibalism, with animal and human sacrificial practices or their substitutes in formalized regions and with the world-wide scalping, head-hunting, body mutilating and necrophilic practices of mankind in proclaiming this common blood-lust differentiator, this predaceous habit, this mark of Cain that separates man dietetically from his anthropoidal relatives and allies him rather with the deadliest of Carnivora."[10]

The chronicles of human aggression[11] paint a pervasive picture that begins with the earliest human-induced animal extinctions during the Pleistocene. Many hundreds of mammal species—and no doubt as yet unrecognized avians and rodents—disappeared in Africa, Europe, North and South America during this period as a result of male hunting forays.

Throughout recorded time, successive waves of warrior barbarians and despots unleashed monumental carnage, leaving piles of skulls, flayed victims, hearts ripped out of living chests, pyramids of bones. Every century, nearly every nation, can be seen to have taken part in this free-for-all of unceasing madness.

Is there a gene for revenge, for slaughter, for hatred? An estimated four million boys and girls were sacrificed by the Aztecs, some 55 a day. They were burned alive, tortured, sexually molested and thrown dismembered into wells and off cliffs. Compare such distant data with the more recent description of a single night along the Merderet River in Normandy, June 1944: "The slaughter once started could not be stopped...Having slaughtered every German in sight, they ran on into the barns of the French farmhouses where they killed the hogs, cows and sheep. The orgy ended when the last beast was dead."[12] In this century, well over 100 million people have been murdered, in addition to several hundred billion, possibly even trillions of animals.

If, as some have argued, we are able to learn from our mistakes, to rationally select our future, why is it that between 1945 and 1976, 25 million people died in 133 wars?

At the same time, investigators have shown that at least 40 percent of the human population has always been engaged in peace. The debate over whether violence is genetic and instinctive, or deliberated and contingent, loses its importance in terms of nomenclatural analysis. Darwin spoke of "monstrosities" that were liable to mutation and speciation. He was speaking of biological formations, like a fin, or a hand. Why not biological ideas?

My point is this: The ideas of good and evil, of violence, of the idea and ideal of nature, like the idea of compassion, and of love, have become their own species. Naturalists, as well. Perhaps also Democrats, Republicans, military minds, economists, Pro-Choicers, astronomers, artists. I do not mean to stint on the possibilities any more than 19th century naturalists stinted on the range of special diversity. Meditation is certainly one method by which this conceptual evolution takes place; whereby an individual can mentally will himself into some other being, some other animal. Darwin wrote, "It is so easy to hide our ignorance under such expressions as the 'plan of creation,' (or) 'unity of design,' &c."[13] What he meant, of course, was that these grand unifying principles were merely excuses, postponements, ways of avoiding the confrontation with a diverse Self.

When Jean-Jacques Rousseau wrote his "Discourse on the Origin of Inequality[14]," he clearly understood the evolutionary power of certain ideas. His celebration of natural thinking was really the apotheosis of "natural man," of a species of thought that was the overriding characteristic of a species of individual, an historical personage whom Rousseau revered. In summoning that character-type, the Swiss philosopher yearned for a revivification of those qualities of perception and ideals which, to his way of thinking, had empowered the noble savage with a more charismatic and compelling personality—even physiology—than could be found among the 19th century Europeans. Rousseau likened himself to something of a primitive throwback. He liked to take long walks in the woods and incessantly idealized the past. But he was not altogether convincing to his peers. When Voltaire read "Discourse," he wrote to Rousseau, "It makes one feel like walking on all fours, when one reads your work. However, it being more than sixty years since I lost the habit, I feel unfortunately that it is impossible for me to get it back, and I leave that natural gait to those who are worthier of it than you or I."[15]

But Darwin fully understood that *gait*. When he returned to England in 1836 from his five year voyage as naturalist on the H.M.S. Beagle, having meditated at length on the peculiar birds, lizards and tortoises of the Galapagos Islands, he was certain that all species underwent evolution. Like Rousseau, whose own theories in this realm were published the year of Darwin's birth, the notion that mutation and descent through generations had altered earlier, mutable forms, made astonishing sense to Darwin.

Both Darwin and Rousseau intimated the possibility of a condition whereby *Homo sapiens* were capable of proliferating into other species.

This is, in essence, conceptual reincarnation in this life. A firm belief in the power of thought. Some Native American Indians are conversant in their customs and mythology with as many as fifteen different sexual genders.[16] Paleo-Siberian shamans in Siberia, up until their assimilation in the last century, were comfortable with the idea of human transmigration into animal souls. Ancient Near Easterners, Egyptians and Greeks were no less aware of these incarnations, from Osiris and Mithra to Cybele and Gaia. A vast treasury of ethnographic and spiritual literature supports inter-special relations which far exceed the limited confines of an anthropocentric biological inquiry. Throughout Asian mythology, animals and humans are constantly merging.

Nevertheless, in contemplating this notion, one is apt to reject the premise that there are human aliens among us, for that is precisely what the theory indicates. "Alien" is not the right word, however. Nor is sub-species, an expression used routinely by Linnaeus and Darwin. The Audubon Society field guides refer to "accidental species" and perhaps this most closely approximates the notion I have in mind. Not surprisingly, the first Pelagic "accidental species" mentioned in the *Guide to North American Birds* happens to be the *Diomedea exulans*, or Wandering Albatross.

The varieties of mental opposition within man that so threaten this planet, whist giving rise to such hope, are indications of different beasts at work; different organisms whose outlook and destiny, whose choices and approaches to the world are built up over a lifetime of inner thought. By thinking of these people—people all around us—as different animals, I sense greater, not lesser opportunities for concord. By reinvesting the diversity of thought with the same dignity and integrity which some would allow the natural world, we reinstate the individual with his and her own animal psyche, individualism, uniqueness.

I'm not sure how, in scientific jargon, to classify people who are...different? Since everyone *is* different. It's not a new classification that I'm looking for. But rather, an end to classifications. Let differences prevail and be justly celebrated; separate but whole. Unalike but unified by certain key traits: a will to live, to see our ideals, our children, our parents, our friends and communities blossom; to witness a human renaissance of compassion that has encompassed the whole world.

There is no point seeking unity, per se, in the guise of global consensus, universal peace and majority rule, at the expense of individuals or of individual species. Indeed, the unity of which I speak should cost nothing. There are no losers in this kind of peace. The words themselves are just words, quotients of the mass and mob, smokescreens which conceal enormous diversity, participles of a species that long ago fragmented into differences. Writes Darwin, "The mind cannot possibly grasp the full meaning of the term of even a million years; it cannot add up and perceive the full effects of many slight variations, accumulated during an almost infinite number of generations."[17]

Better, then, to acknowledge openly all the taxing, contradictory, marvelous variations, the ethical, cerebral, aesthetic, attitudinal differences that are as day and night, as different animal species altogether. That way, at least, we know where we stand. Not before brick walls with whom debate might turn rancorous or violent, but before miraculous beings, mothers and daughters, fathers and sons—as graceful as snow leopards and macaws; as indelicate, perhaps, as murderers and madmen—but with whom we have a lot of tolerant, probing discussion and catching up to accomplish.[18]

In short, what I am proposing is that we put aside our similarities—we've already been through that—and instead celebrate our differences!

[1]George William Foote, editor of *Free Thinker*, 1904, in *Vision and Realism - A Hundred Years of The Free Thinker*, by Jim Herrick, p. 33, G. W. Foote & Co., London 1982.

[2]See *Biology—It's Principles And Implications*, by Garrett Hardin and Carl Bajema, W. H. Freeman And Co., San Francisco, 1978, p. 366.

[3]The oldest known example of manipulated fire comes from the region of Mount Kenya, at a location called Chesowanja. There, scientists located remains of Homo erectus dating to 1.4 million years ago.

[4]See the author's work, *After Eden—History, Ecology & Conscience*, San Diego, Avant Books, 1986 p. 24.

[5]*On The Origin Of Species by Means of Natural Selection, or the Preservation of Favored Races in the Struggle for Life*, With a New Preface by Charles G. Darwin, The Easton Press, 1976, p. 34-35.

[6]ibid., Darwin, p. 31.

[7]ibid., Darwin, p. 40.

[8] ibid., Darwin, p. 44.

[9]ibid., Darwin, p. 380.

[10]"The Predatory Transition from Ape to Man," *International Anthropological and Linguistic Review*, 1 (1953).

[11]See John Keegan and Joseph Darracott's *The Nature of War*, New York: Holt, Rinehard & Winston, 1981; Quincy Wright's *A Study of War*, 2nd ed., Chicago: University of Chicago Press, L. Dawidowicz's *The War Against The Jews, 1933-1945*, New York: Bantam Books, 1976; J. Glenn Gray's *The Warriors: Reflections on Men in Battle*, New York: Harper & Row, 1967; Freidrich Nietzsche's *The Will to Power: An Attempted Transvaluation of All Values*, London, 1913; Arnold Toynbee's *Mankind and Mother Earth—A Narrative History of the World,* New York: Oxford University Press, 1976; Irenaus Eibl Eibesfeldt's *The Biology of Peace and War: Men, Animals, and Aggression*, trans. by E. Mosbacher, New York: Viking Press, 1979; and Sue Mansfield's *The Gestalts of War: An Inquiry into Its Origins and Meanings as a Social Institution*, New York: The Dial Press, 1982.

[12]S.L.A. Marshall, *Men Against Fire*, New York: William Morrow, 1947.

[13]op.cit., Darwin, p.438.

[14]Jean-Jacques Rousseau, "Discours sur l'origine de l'inegalite," in *Oeuvres completes de Jean-Jacques Rousseau*, ed. Pleiade Bernard Gagnebin and Marcel Raymond, Paris, 1959.

[15]See L. G. Crocker's *Rousseau's Social Contract: An Interpretive Essay*, Cleveland: Case Western Reserve University Press, 1968.

[16]One psychologist, Dr. Maureen O'Hara, has identified 47 different genderal and sexual types among *Homo Sapiens*. "Futurist Conference," MCA-Universal, June 1, 1993. In addition, Nobel Prize winner Manfred Eigen of the Max Planck Institute for Biophysical Chemistry in Götingen, Germany, has devised the name "quasispecies" for those creatures, like human immunodeficiency virus (HIV) that "evolve a million times faster than cellular microorganisms." See "Viral Quasispecies," by Manfred Eigen, Scientific American, July 1993, pp. 42-49.

[17]op.cit., Darwin, p. 438.

[18]In acknowledging that a species requires at least a hundred thousand years to change (a fact of charged relevance for *Homo sapiens*, who are fast approaching that very birthday) Frederick Turner trenchantly asks, "Would it not be better if something like Lamarckian evolution were to supplement Darwinian evolution?—an adaptive process that could make appreciable changes in one generation, which could use the experience of individuals rather than that of the gene pool as a whole? Would not evolution be still more efficient if alternative scenarios for the future could be tried out in a virtual world where they could do no damage, before they were actually embarked on?" See Turner's book, *Beauty—The Value of Values*, pp. 124-125, University Press of Virginia, 1991. Some scientists have given the name "chronospecies" to a population which becomes a new species over time. "Chronospeciation" would thus describe the process of population diversification.

IX
The Mind In An Age of Ecological Stress

Suddenly, no at last, long last I couldn't anymore, I couldn't go on...
How can I go on, I shouldn't have begun.
No, I had to begin.[1]

—*Samuel Beckett*

This is a meditation on what I am calling "true consciousness." With all of the turmoil surrounding any cognizant individual, there must be some thoughts more given to resolution, release and stability than others. With that simplistic premise in mind, I attempt to follow a path of integral awareness that is neither shy nor blind. With awareness comes recovery.

"A pperception" is a word that always absorbed me, from childhood, which is when I first began thinking about it, about that capacity of the human intellect to focus on its own thought processes. Apperception connotes a meditative technique par excellence, not merely in its literal ability to perceive perception, but by its liberated point of view, which enables it to stand back from the avalanche of life, from information pollution, and to gaze in a pure state of awareness. We spend our days perceiving things. But the faint, distant, inner awareness that we are, in fact, perceiving, is its own perceptual universe, with gradations and latitudes. Try it: indwell the mind at work, the mind at play. Feel the luminous weight of extraterritorial awareness bearing down on the everyday. Visualize that freedom, stepping back from the perceptual clutter and static. Where can one go with that pure awareness? It seems unbound, a layer of consciousness almost never used, like a heavy wool suit in the tropics or silk slacks in the Arctic.

But there is another way to consider our apperceptive possibilities. Remember that the same evolutionary brain responsible for so much rampant destruction is highly attuned to its own deeds and misfortunes; is ensnared in a dark night of contrition that acknowledges, heeds warnings, mumbles theory and poetry to itself; argues, delineates, scorns, diverts attention from, but does little or nothing, ultimately, to inhibit its brilliant malignancy. Taken together, these ironies constitute a brave new forlorn world. The malaise—like that of any depression—is wont to sink deeper and deeper into itself, nearly always preferring the status quo to the unknown. But the awareness of this condition possesses the seed of reversal, and we are gaining evidence of that turn-around every day in the world.

Psychiatry has treated mental health issues and personal breakdowns for centuries. The question that raises itself is this: How does such awareness deal with adversity which is bigger than oneself? When it has become environmental? The byproduct of one's own species? What are the options for an aware happiness and what are the ways to get there? Awareness breeds more, not less, awareness. The problems would seem to compound themselves in the mind, until awareness becomes benumbed, its vigor and means of combating crisis sapped from within. In his trenchant analysis of mankind's habituation to nuclear weapons (in *The Fate of the Earth*), Jonathan Schell referred to the sluggishness of a nervous system that had, for too long, become inured to such a prospect. The prospect of ineluctable environmental decay, like the presence of nuclear weapons, has induced generation after generation—at least since the period of the Industrial

Revolution during the late 18th century—into this habitual, melancholic mindset of futility and anger.

The Earth, a victim, all-vulnerable, has given rise to no such dilemma. But the Mind, which carries the immediate burden of its ruminations to bed each night—between fits of fleeting satisfaction, laughter and forgetting—must wonder: What is really happening? How can I break out of the syndrome?

Some families sit around at night and count their blessings, like merchants tallying their revenues at the end of each day. Their aggravation does not leave the confines of their business or their immediate family needs. This is a way out. Saying a prayer at dinner, delighting in the family, are other ways out. Positive approaches to living. Becoming involved. Taking a stance. Aspiring towards change.

Such needed changes are everywhere about us. One need only open one's eyes. When Mahatma Gandhi opened *his* eyes, he saw a bleeding humanity and chose almost at once to plunge his family blessings and personal gain into India's enormous sea of suffering. He founded a commune, simplified his life, wrote down his thoughts and utilized the many jail cells into which he was tossed as sources of increasing self-assurance and meditation. Gandhi's vision entailed the moral, political and economic liberation of all Indians.

By contrast, today's ecological open-eyes confront an even more daunting invocation. Here are just a few of those scenarios:

1) Something like 100 billion animals are tortured and murdered throughout the world, every year. The hideously diverse reasons are one and the same.

2) Worldwide, as many as 60 percent of all living species are being catapulted to extinction as a result of that same cause; call it human greed, evil or sheer laziness. Evolution normally casts about 300 species to extinction every million years. Today, one species, man, has been responsible for possibly fifteen million extinctions—trillions of animals, plants and insects—in less than one century.

3) More than 270,000 human children are needlessly dying of starvation every week.

4) A thin layer of toxic petroleum covers most of the planet. In just one city, New York, there are over 10,000 oil and chemical spills every year.

5) Carcinogenic DDT residues are routinely found in all mother's milk—whether mare, grizzly or human—in every country, on every continent. DDT, like acid rain, obeys no international boundaries.

6) In farms and ranches in South America, New Zealand and Australia, hoofed animals are going blind because of man-made chlorofluorocarbons in the upper stratosphere. In a Florida zoo, the same upper ozone depletion is blinding a white Bengal tiger.

7) A Sunday edition of many major city newspapers results in the destruction of 60 more acres of hardwood. Meanwhile, half the forests of North America have been wiped out in the last 150 years. In Thailand, Nepal and India, nearly 95 percent of all forests are gone.

8) Most of the world's crucial estuaries, wetlands and mangroves, are being destroyed by real estate development, unchecked urban growth and landfills.

9) A Silverback Gorilla is being tortured by its "owner" in a concrete cage in a shopping mall in Seattle. The animal has been trapped there for thirty years.

10) A third of all fruit and produce consumed by Americans is imported from abroad, where there are few if any controls on toxic pesticides. Indeed, American industry is encouraged to sell its unwanted poisons to foreign countries, despite the knowledge that our own children are consuming the end-products.

11) The U.S. government has now secretly approved new transgenic procedures whereby animal genes will be crossed with plant genes to create new, supposedly enriched, plants. There will be no labels to warn vegetarians of these genetic mutants. Indeed, Congress has disregarded the tens of millions of vegetarians in the United States.

12) The fertility of the North American soil has been diminished by half since the Puritans first landed on these shores.

13) Not a single river in the United States is safe to drink from or swim in.

15) While writing this book, 28 people, mostly under the age of 30, were gunned down and murdered in separate incidents in Los Angeles during the third weekend in August, 1992.

The litany of ecological assaults, contradictions and cumulative schizophrenia is mounting. The arguments engulfing such statistics are wearisome. There is little possibility of convincing anyone of a fact or attitude who does not want to change his or her mind on a given issue. Half the world seems focused on these crises; the other half does not.

How, then, does an aware individual cope with the realization that his own indecisive, overpopulated, out-of-control species is the culprit? One cannot become an expatriot and move to Paris. We are stuck with the fact that people are people. There is no escaping ourselves. Suicide is no solution. We're already committing suicide. That is not a useful answer.

That leaves the individual condemned to feeling rage; an anger, or despair, which wells up from a wound that will not heal; from abuse that is getting worse; from a collective unconscious which is becoming every day more unconscious for all of its supposed awareness.

Take a poll, sample strangers on the street and they will almost unanimously share your frustration, your hurt, your worry. Most of my less high and mighty friends take humanity's oppression of Nature very personally. But then, if my friends (and your friends) are not the guilty ones, who is? Who, exactly, is this "humanity" that is always thrown up as the culpable, schizophrenic madman on the loose? A psychotic killer who would rather have cardboard boxes than redwood forests? Who are those "unaware" people? And are they any more guilty than the supposedly "aware" ones? We *all* think it's the other guy's fault. That's one of the problems.

This query is self-evident. The human species is culpable. And this is problematic. Because saying that we're all guilty—that we all trespass on other creatures' turf; pollute, consume, contribute, in short, to the overall problem—won't get us anywhere. Pointing the finger at certain alleged bad guys is also no remedy, only a child's temper tantrum.

We are now living in a state of perpetual ecological disaster. Ecological disaster requires amelioration, psychological mending, after-shock therapy. What are the therapies that can help people—and by inference, the planet—to heal, to become whole and happy and creatively fulfilled? And by what inward process of conflict resolution, imaginative ordeal and self-help can that transition come about? More importantly, how—in an era of widespread pain and shock valuelessness—can an individual become truly happy, without guilt? Buddha, of course, addressed this very same query. His resulting Eight Fold Path preached gentleness and increasing renunciation. But Buddhism, it would appear, has scarcely affected the course of wars and human misery, any more than Christianity, with its equally vigorous affirmation of love, has had much of an impact on human cruelty, or humanity's penchant to go astray. Some crucial, inner part of the equation is lacking.

I say *inner* because one can describe solutions, celebrate exemplars, educate others, even lead horses to water, but it appears to be a biological principle that a horse will only drink if it's good and ready.

By thus predicating an inward enterprise, I am not discounting Golden Rules, Ten Commandments, universal ethics of all kinds, but rather seeking ways to bolster those injunctions, to exalt inner strength, the ideas and passions which must ultimately express themselves in the world and complete the logical circle. Without a coherent, poetic, and gently aware inward being, there is little hope of manifesting relationships that are based upon innocence as opposed to guilt.

There are certainly levels of innocence and guilt, of compromise and excess, that can be looked at. For example, the near destruction of the Persian Gulf marine environment was the calculated doing of a few men in power in Iraq—an example of unimaginable stupidity. But there were other equally tormented conspirators in Germany and the U.S., and elsewhere in the Middle East; nations which had calculated that arming Iraq against Iran was the more expedient, the more profitable of two evils. This was an example of an international relationship devoid of true ethical context.

Innocence and guilt operate not just among nations, but at home. They are states at the heart of the meditation process.

A philosophy of innocence means that whatever gives rise to guilt is wrong. Whatever threatens the existence of diverse life forms (however subtly), whatever perpetrates knowing cruelty, is also guilt-driven and translates into ecological impact.

The whole point of environmental meditation is in seeking to discover not the whole world, in all its endless disputes and alliances, breaths and breathlessness, but that *particular* which may engender a renaissance in the human heart to minimize violence, and thus to alleviate guilt and the environmental stress of which it is a part.

It means mending the human world by personal vows and personal growth. These are not narrow categories, dour and defensive, but tolerant blessings, meant to foster love, diversity and community patience. And which, of necessity and out of joy, must translate into action.

Finally, it makes no sense to love one species and hate another. This disposition is any dictator's big personality shortcoming. A tragic flaw that leads possibly good people to behave like idiots and oil spills; to pit their own beliefs against all others. It disables any possibility of constructive dialogue, alternative points of view, of tolerance. Tolerance is the key to evolution. Its most wondrous expression is biodiversity—which happens to be the only sensible ecological ethic on Earth.

We are supremely loquacious. Human beings have the gift of gab. But with over 100 million murders in the 20th century, thus far, our dialogue is apparently lacking something critical, not only to the well-being of the world, but to ourselves, who supposedly understand the languages we wield with one another. What is the problem?

It is the inner dialogue which is incomplete or entirely lacking. It's one thing to be rhetorically efficient, blustering, legalistic, dynamic, even eloquent, on the outside. But that's too easily a mere show, an expedient ruse. Politics and business. The deal-making which has come to resemble some Orwellian world of obtuse nuance and half-truth. What counts is the inward maturity, the voice of conscience and reason, deeply thought out, patiently expressed, lived with gratitude and a profound awareness that life is tragically brief but abundantly beautiful. Short of these professions, this ecopsychology, we are but living embodiments of what the French philosopher, Jean-Paul Sartre, called "false consciousness."

[1]Samuel Beckett, *Texts for Nothing* (New York: Grove Press, 1962.)

X
EcoPsychology

You never enjoy the world aright till the sea itself floweth in your veins,
till you are clothed with the heavens and crowned with the stars;
and perceive yourself to be the sole heir of the whole world, and more
then so, because men are in it who are every one sole heirs as well as you.

—Thomas Traherne[1]

Ecology—when viewed from the perspective of psychoanalysis—reverts forcefully back to its original Greek meaning, which was "house cleaning." To put one's own immediate surroundings in good order. The environment will be pristine, preserved and sanctified when one's own thoughts and mental horizons are equally so.

In a recent map of remaining planetary wilderness, the human investiture is seen to have spread across more than 50 percent of the Earth's landmass. This is only the obvious measure of our colonization, of course. The image a satellite is likely to yield of cities, rural habitation, drainage culverts, phantom forests, marine "dead zones" and chemical blooms, freeways, skyscrapers, and burning rain forests are all signs of human population density. But if one includes the spread of contaminants in the air and soil and water, lead poisoning in the blood of wild mustangs, cataracts in Patagonian guanacos or traces of radioactivity in the Tibetan yak, then our ecological imperialism takes on ever more dramatic dimensions.

Beyond these gross physical indicators of the human presence, however, is a psychological one: the mental homesteads, barbed wires, ethical impostures and psychic annexations of the whole world. The human brain seeks companionship in the wild, even as it trudges to work amid concrete and steel, driven by contrary inclinations whose roots are hormonal, verbal, of the hypothalamus, in other words.

My mind is immersed in the gigantic, historical distraction of settlement and survival: eating and sleeping, elimination, family, the sky, the sun and the moon. Daily, I have a mental picture of dental floss and accountability, of teapots and diapers. The struggle for jobs, the disappointment with other people, lost opportunities; those eternally shuffling crowds. All around me, in me, is the power of an alien social force which impinges century after century on lives that are essentially brief and unfulfilled. I know that. I have memories of an eternal childhood which is gone. I harbor a belief in certain liberties that are jeopardized, a hope of something which is only a hope, undefined, typically defiled. And I sense that universal search in myself for an ephemeral beauty—mysterious and unnameable—that arises under conditions of extreme unhappiness, claustrophobia and congestion; or, conversely, as the result of complacence, compliance or unintelligibility. Or, finally, I dance the dance of joy, led on by the sheer exhuberance of a life, any life, which is mine for a day.

Something like 600 million visits per year are now paid to parks and national forests in the United States. People need nature. The back to nature movements of the past 3000 years (for that's how long, at the very least, such nostalgia has played an active role in the human imagination) are characterized by this ecopsychological requirement. Ancient Roman writers like Vergil in his *Georgics* longed for an escape to the country and mocked the infestation of big city ways—filth, noise, crime.

But prior to this expression of a deep-seated naturalism, there is evidence that early Mesolithic and late Paleolithic artisans were obsessed with a different back-to-nature evocation. By depicting a variety of animals, some half-human, in the guise of all-powerful deities, these first painters hinted at the roots of mental disassociation or schizophrenia; at what some speculative psychiatrists, engrossed in the history of human maladaption, have termed the bicameral mind. This pertains to that threshold of human gatherings where the social comforts and mental reckonings of the collective had begun quite significantly to take the place of human oneness with nature. By implication, the earliest cities, be they cave cultures, had accelerated the disassociation. Language itself, and the general web of certitudes it propounds, all worked to repudiate the quality of being spellbound. Early human habitation found a way around some of life's physical difficulties, captured, tamed, destroyed, multiplied, mutilated; peered straight into the new day by way of muscle and conquest without an inkling of remorse or humility.

The ancient artist recorded this hubris. He, or she was like some weathervane, reading the advancing winds of civilization and measuring the disquiet. These artists alluded to a growing question mark in the human psyche. The study of ancient art—from what is today Namibia to aboriginal China—suggests a formidable pattern of angst in the visible signs of a yearning for that lost or mythological past.

The price of such loss was one of dsyfunctionalism, of innumerable cultures whose mental health simply broke down in the wake of massive environmental ruination. As these societies waged campaigns against the physical world—stripping hillsides, diverting water, extracting building materials, engineering new worlds—so did the campaigns turn on one another. In the Near East and Mediterranean, in the Mayan uplands, throughout Southeast Asia, the emergence of civilization almost always harnessed nature, as it turned with psychotic violence against itself. The management of this manipulative and ultimately self-destructive frenzy in the human collective is what we have always termed politics. It is a form of privilege intent upon sacrifice, a system of imperatives with no priority, the apotheosis of comfort far beyond what the body itself requires. This accumulative delusion of stability we call wealth. But it is actually a disease. There are currently 202 known billionaires, over three million millionaires, and several billion poor and homeless people.

In the midst of economic disparity and unhealthy minds, we attempt today to put back together the shards of a broken contract. To resurrect what must have been, and must always be, a most delicate relationship with nature, prior to the gang and the worship of money.

Can a sick person heal himself in the heart of the mass to which we are connected? The question keeps recurring in different guises. There are countless medical, religious and soft energy metaphors that might serve in this design. For example, the doctor's proverbial "get lots of rest and drink plenty of fluids" has the right blend of benign and meditative potions to shake off the bulk of human maladies. The spiritualist calling, with its voluntary simplification, its stripping bare of life's unessentials, its act of reverence for awareness and creation, also harkens back to gentler, healthier times. The alternative energy scenario, with its "50 ways to save the planet," can be read by children and may, no doubt, enable us to extend the distance between two points.

Yet none of these remedies are truly psychological. But it is in the mind where the problem is born and continues to fester. Furthermore, in the deep rifts of big city anxiety, such antidotes have become vacuous platitudes of the New Age.

EcoPsychology implies a divisive shift in the grammar of narcissism. While the term does not propose to alter the personal preoccupations or indwelling with which mental trauma is associated, it *does* focus upon a larger sphere of connections than mere Self. EcoPsychology relates to the interconnectedness of all beings, to the vulnerability of those connections, and to the breakdown in mind and body which will occur when those connections are severed. A third of all Westerners will suffer fits of intense depression throughout their lives; medical depression that often results in other serious illnesses, in a constant state of unhappiness, in debilitating guilt, in violence to others, and finally, in suicide. All as a result of that fragile conceptual connection to the outside having been cut off.

Some epidemiologists have likened depression syndromes to a national paroxysm, and the numbers of afflicted are increasing rapidly. There are drugs one can take to soften depression, but no drug can reverse certain volatile assumptions that are inherent to mental breakdown. They include the following premises, matters of habitual acceptance that have begun to prove untenable, impossible to embrace or uphold, or utterly abhorrent to what at least some human hearts are feeling:

1. Namely, that human beings are in control.

2. That *Homo sapiens* have inalienable God-given rights over nature, simply on account of their mental and physical abilities to exploit and manipulate.

3. That we are brighter and better than all other animal and plant species.

4. That, for better or for worse, we must do what we must do.

5. That the human animal will never change.

6. That it would be a fate worse than death to have to suffer the poverty, the ennui, the desperate ignorance and superstition of our ancestors.

7. That things are just going to get worse and worse, more and more complicated, and it's probably our own fault.

8. That nature is cruel, unreliable, indifferent.

9. That if you think cities are bad, try the Serengeti.

10. That there are far more homeless ants than homeless people.

11. Human life, in other words, is superior to life in general.

12. And finally, human beings have collectively transcended nature.

Countless other assumptions, political or ethical dispositions, contradictory decrees, admissions of ideological custom, arrogance, fear, hatred, even—in rare and most frightening cases—actual conviction, escalate the gulf which separates a human being from the family of life. And this bifurcation is as physical as it is mental. Our mental maps are implacable; our knowledge and surveys of the world fanatical. The functioning mind will never elude the world. It cannot escape the burden of itself in that world. And so, to talk casually about remedy, salvation, the re-attunement of balance, is to embark upon a fantastic undertaking that is liable to daunt the most ardent aspirant.

Yet we all aspire, nevertheless. We are going on more and more pilgrimages, seeking more and more power, using more words, music, money and energy to reach that place of ecological balance and subsequent mental well-being than ever before. Whatever differences sunder the rich and the poor, the different races, cultures, and religious groups, the Democrats and Republicans, one unifying recognition holds all of us hostage: the rather prevailing sense that a polluted mind pollutes the environment which in turn pollutes our bodies. A similar message was coined by the Japanese sage Kukai ("The Mother of Japanese Civilization") over a thousand years ago: "The environment changes in function with the mind: if the mind is filthy, the environment will be polluted. But also the mind is influenced by the environment: when the surroundings are quiet, the mind becomes calm. Thus mind and environment meet in an invisible manner, like the Tao and the virtuous efficiency which resides in the Obscure."[2] The ring of Kukai's message has stretched to the end of the millennium, where we now must again confront its truth. There is no chicken/egg riddle to unsort. The arithmetic is brutal: we violate ourselves through the medium of a vulnerable biosphere. And we do so as the result of several thousands of generations of increasingly self-obsessed indulgence. Is there any other way to live? Is human self-obsession (why not call it self-interest?) any different from other species' will to survive? Who has the right, or the wisdom, to distinguish survival from pleasure? And what difference does it make? What's wrong with pleasure, and whose business is it, anyway?

The basis by which EcoPsychology might become relevant to real people's lives is not easily organized or worked out. Even the language one uses to describe it is suffused with imperfect analogies, opinions that are personal, naive or simply inaccurate.

Furthermore, neither history nor the future is necessarily all good or all bad. Not everyone eats meat, builds skyscrapers or willfully kills or pollutes. As members of a biological community, like it or not, we are tied to hundreds of trillions of parts. The first man and the first woman were denizens of a massive natural city that lacked interstate banks and overpasses but made up for it in beaver lodges and termite dens. In parts of Africa, those dens are cone-shaped, often forty feet high, containing populations which exceed the human populations of Calcutta or Tokyo. If an African termite is, say, half-an-inch tall, those cones are equivalent to New York apartment highrises the size of the Empire State Building. Is there some uncanny message in that? I hope not.

Suppose there is a biological equivalency between species which shoots to hell all ecological piety. Suppose, as I have often wondered, that the attrition rates of war, mental and physical disease, over-population and human-induced pollution, are all part of a game plan crucial to the planet's vitality? Would EcoPsychology then be in vain? A futile and chronic case of whining with no basis in reality, only in the spoiled child's fantasy world?

I don't know. We are our own devil's advocates; gifted with rhetoric, with polemic and ambiguity; eager to assemble here, and demolish there; defenders and prosecutors capable of arguing every position, justifying any behavior or indicting the least intention. Occasionally, though it is rare, we even change our minds.

But however one wishes to view the deck of history and human behavior—stacked against nature, or stacked against ourselves—the odds in favor of disaster or amelioration are remarkably the same. And that's the bottom line, no matter how the argument catches you.

All of the medieval theological disputes pertaining to destiny and free will are once again in vogue. This time, however, the issue is not whether God exists, and if so, is he merciful, is he ruthless; is she shy and silent, or meddling and boisterous. The issue, the burning question, is whether there is even a humanity or a human being?

And if so, what is its role in the world?

Each individual claims his or her individuality. Each of us bathes in the psychic pools of ourselves, lounging in the tropical, far-off waters of our own private self-image. We need basics, a fact that seems unlikely to ever change. And those basics are contained in the world to varying degrees. And so the interaction of the person and the Earth is an invariant.

But beyond that basic rule, the mind configures and choreographs all else. EcoPsychology, which is obviously applicable to all species with minds, with self-interest and willfulness, is a test of our tolerance. An urging to become true to ourselves, to become something, or someone, that perhaps we are not; an injunction to evolve, perhaps; or to be more forgiving, or merciful, or kind; to think more carefully about what we really need and don't need, and to be considerate of others. Not just of other people, though that is essential, but of the grass, and the little bugs in the grass. Not that it is mandatory that everyone love bugs. Surely it is not (though it would be nice). But because somehow, over thousands of years, the accumulation of our biases and prejudices has come back to haunt us. There are so many ghosts in our brains that we can't even begin to name them all or sort them out. Our unconscious wells with the maelstrom of aversions; our egos and ids and dreams runneth over with impropriety; and with the egos, ids and dreams of those countless strangers, genetically linked, that came before us.

The sum total of these psychic deficits and avowals we know to be civilization, with its discontents and glories. It's big stuff, removed from the way the mind ordinarily operates, shopping for groceries or driving the kids to school or playing basketball.

And yet, at the same time, no activity, no moment of the day is without a natural context, the relational quintessence of nature to our thoughts. The mind seeks all around itself, gently setting sail into a sea of constant new possibilities, toward mental islands off the known map. Islands of health and dignity and beauty. Which is where the next millennium must chart its course. These are the mental maps of EcoPsychology.

[1]Thomas Traherne, *Centuries of Meditation*, quoted in Thomas Merton, *Mystics and Zen Masters*, p. 133, New York: Farrar, Straus & Giroux, 1967.
[2]From Kukai's "Stone Inscription for the Sramana Shodo Who Crossed the Mountains and Streams in His Search for Awakening," translated by Allan Grapard, in *The Mountain Spirit*, edited by Michael Tobias and Harold Drasdo, p. 54, Victor Gollanecz Ltd., London, 1980.

XI
A Morning At Chartres

See no diversity in yourself when you pray, and let your intelligence take on the impression of no form; but go immaterially to the immaterial and you will understand...

—Evagrius Ponticus[1]

In the religious light of a great cathedral, there is a contagion of sumptuous meta-
phors for our own inner thoughts. Where greatness merges with an ideal; where
nature's fondest whims coalesce in homage to the spirit, impulses played out in the
anonymous hands that once built such a structure; in the universal biology of
creation that engendered those hands and hearts in the first place. The psychic
journey back into time is timeless at a place like Chartres.

I magine the splendid medieval edifice, piercing the medieval sky, the modern sky. Medieval eyes. Modern eyes. What difference, the sky being the sky, human eyes being human eyes? But the *idea* of history. The picture one is willing to compose of it. And the message that has accumulated therein.

Oddly, for our time, that history can be read according to two diver-gent paths. We can see an increasing trend towards self-aggrandizement and infliction, or pay witness to the soft stride towards empathy. The casual observer can remark upon ancient revelation and its systematic degradation, or, preferably, highlight those self-sustaining Ideals which have never fal-tered.

For myself, Chartres is one of those Ideals. One may object: a cathe-dral, man-made, distorts the true purpose of stone, which is to remain where it was created, not to be hewn and hacked and re-assembled like some Brueghelesque Tower of Babel, bursting over the landscape, an ungainly symbol of mankind's vanity and dissolution here on Earth. Such a cathedral destroys the otherwise unblemished horizon, forces the eye unnaturally to focus on a narrow ideological center, where previously, the whole of nature was the center, generously open to all, not merely to those Christians who welcomed an anachronistic Beyond. And finally, the price of creating such monuments must arouse a certain suspicion, if not an outright hostility, for while there were people hungry and poor and uneducated all around Chartres, here was the Church erecting yet another monument to God at great cost.

Similar arguments can be used to decry other engineering chimeras, like a space station, or the would-be hydroelectric plant once destined to irrevocably alter the wilderness of Dinosaur National Monument. The victory over that dam, won by outraged citizens who were not intimidated by an august array of government forces pushing for its construction, signaled the first political precedent for a successful wilderness activism in the United States. How is Chartres any different than a dam, some might be resolved to ask? The inherent proposition holds that all construction must stop, that mankind has seen enough material progress, too many roads, automobiles, people, supermarkets, high buildings, and too little natural habitat.

I am all for that proposition, 100 percent, but am inclined to add that Chartres was constructed at a time when there were *not* too many supermarkets or automobiles; when the Christians who erected the cathedral believed, I suspect, that they—every man, woman and child—were partaking in a great work of art which would inspire generations to come. It gave them jobs, a sense of dignity, a pride in place, and a continuity altogether French which dates back to the first settlers hundreds of thousands of years ago, at a lovely spot called Terra Amata, in present day Nice, where the original Frenchmen erected little huts with indoor bathrooms overlooking the Mediterranean. Prime real estate. Even then, the French excelled in the aesthetic realm. Later, at caves like that of Lascaux, haunted by ecstatic wonderment and the rituals of priests and artisans, the French sense of the sacred grew up and prospered.

Chartres evolved out of a tradition of love, a sense of this eternal mystery. The cathedral may be about God, but it is as much about nature, in the broadest, grandest sense.

And it was always thus. In ancient Greece and Rome, ideas about the Divine and the natural were interchangeable. For the Epicureans, for Cicero and Lucretius and Vergil, for nearly every thinker worth his salt, Mother Earth was construed as *the* fundamental concept. And, as concept, she changed all subsequent thinking, meant everything, was familiar to everyone. Hippocrates and Thales connected the health of the individual with the health of the planet. Plotinus, a neo-Platonist, envisioned a universal natural soul. Seneca chided the construction industry for erecting "towering tenements" that were counter to Mother Earth, and pitted the city and its multitudes against the philosophical, serene, anti-technological rural lifestyle.

We may believe that our modern wisdom grants us certain engineering priorities; that we know more than our predecessors. This is true and this is false. Numerous ancient agricultural treatises recognized the importance of maintaining a fertile soil and preventing erosion. Fallow fields, meandering flocks, an ease in all things summoned the sensibility of a Golden Age of Nature, even 2000 years ago. Common sense and spirituality; art and nature; mind and matter: all were considered one.

These unisons flourished both self- and unself-consciously, many centuries before the yearning for a better past entered the modern philosopher's consciousness. Among the desert fathers and earliest saints, the revery of nature had become spiritual, a poetic contemplation that combined the God in every detail with general truths that were aesthetic ones. God's marvels could be read in the landscape, a revelation that achieved its high point during Medieval times in the writings and lives of St. Bernard (1091-1153), St. Francis (1182-1226) and St. Thomas Aquinas (1225-1274), contemporaries of my morning at Chartres. Bernard reveled in the sea; Francis in animals; Thomas in the cosmopolitan character of nature. Every facet of experience prior to the late 18th century industrialization of Europe appears to have been haunted by the joys of their spring, the lowing of their cows, the love psalms of their youth.

Chartres, like the cathedrals at Reims and Notre Dame, and the four monasteries of Citeaux, was built in the spirit of such poets; men and women whose piety was both practical and melodious. A St. Bernard of Clairvaux might take charge of bringing in the hay, working the soil or writing verse. While wild animals took refuge at the churches, befriended the monks and provided ample stories for hagiographic legend. Centaurs, lions, lambs, stags, all the requisite four-legged creatures of the terrestrial paradise, showed up at Chartres and were loved there.

There were sophisticated laws to protect nature, then. The earliest air pollution rulings were in effect in England as early as the 1300's. Germans in the 12th century guarded their *Bannforst*, meaning "reserved forests," from clear cutting. Under King Ludwig of Bavaria, regulations were set forth in 1331 making it a firm policy, both religious and political, that "any act considered harmful to the forest" must be censured. Hotels in France could use a certain amount of wood, "provided they did not reduce the heat of the poor." Choice forests were reserved for hunting grounds; individual consumption of wood, pasture and soil was supervised by local government. Sheep and goat grazing was restricted. Soil was to be fertilized. As early as the 14th century in France, there were reforestation ordinances. Yet it is also important to remember that what was not censured included the exploitation of every species of tree for nearly every household good, from baking trough to axle. The tree was used completely: pine torches, beer mugs, dyes from bark, food from the wild pear. Nothing was wasted.[2]

At the same time, quarrying was considered next to godliness: in the first three centuries of this millennium, the French constructed 580 mighty cathedrals and churches out of stone, not to mention thousands of smaller sized chapels.[3]

Chartres, in more or less its present form, was completed in 1240, a precocious fusion of Romanesque and Gothic aspirations; a technological addiction to heights—both spires exceeding 350 feet. The entire sanctity of the church rests on its alleged possession of the Virgin Mary's robe, somehow left on earth during her Assumption, eventually acquired by Charlemagne and subsequently donated to Chartres by the Emperor's grandson.

Thousands of local volunteers, from a sense of supreme devotion, had helped haul the stones off barges on the river Eure, piously, silently pushing and dragging the masons' carts up the long hill. The communal effort coincided with similar endeavors in Paris, Sens, Senlis, Noyon and across Normandy. But none of these other cathedrals would match the combination of height and stained glass tracery that is Chartres.

The fields of La Beauce all around; the bas-reliefs overhead, compassionate depictions, surrounded by the grass and the wind.

Enter…Walk into the light…

"The wisdom that is moved by the spirit is the power of pure, spiritual, and angelic prayer, whose characteristic consists in this, that the understanding of the one praying becomes perfectly detached from all external things and gives no glance with its material eyes to itself nor anything else, since, by the light that works in it, it has become withdrawn from the world of sense. Then the understanding, inexpressibly united with God in one spirit, frees itself from matter and becomes immaterial and like light…"[4]

That light pours through the clerestory windows of the nave and choir, touching with an ambient stream of photons those smooth acres of stone, plunging directly into mind. The height is defined by the glass, and by the glassy depiction of evangelical visions, kings, saints, prophets and ancient calendrical events associated with farming and cosmology. Vertiginous halos; a verticality of motes pinioned in mid-stream, mid-color. Fitted with a delicate suspension that seems to defy the laws of engineering. Solidity and the bulwarks of reason give way to luster and air, to the translucence of Being and the fragility of this world.

I watch tourists from all countries saunter along the smooth stone palimpsests, gliding over eternity in the ague of a promise that is universal.

Nature's course illuminated. Not modified, but sanctified; neither conquered nor ignored, but rather invested with ourselves.

Soft, cool, historical relationships that warm up almost at once inside myself. This is the music of the spheres, captured in the space of silence. Ascension, Virgins, the Crucifixion, are all relaxed, somehow, in this revelation of quietude. A sketchbook of nature, instinct with the Papacy, with Copernicus, with all the wild physical chants of early Western history, percolates upwards to my lips like a rustic theology. Poetry, teleology, the mystical and the sacred.

These impressions have their possibility for consciousness beyond the sheer delight one must universally feel. The cathedral was meant to instill reverence for God; to promote lasting prayer, penetrating awe, good intentions and good deeds. Forget the hideous contradictions, the murderous Crusades. One must try to separate the achievement of a Chartres from the odious realms of dogma and mortification into which all religious thought has plunged from time to time.

The mission engendered here at Chartres invoked a sense of beauty that far exceeded the sum of its parts. From its very origins in the 11th century, this devotion must have spilled out into the surrounding country, in the poetry of Lent, the music of troubadors, and the aesthetic penchant for all things sacred in France. And among the French whose family farming traditions, everywhere evident in the neighboring countryside, have not diminished much in 800 years. And whose predilection for Impressionist picnics, white tablecloths, fresh vegetables, the grape and the baguette, must be viewed as French mantras, environmental secret passwords. Understand the grape and one is a citizen. Appreciate a white tablecloth, and one will be a part of a community. Produce, or shop for fresh vegetables, and that community is strengthened.

The *dejeuner sur l'herbe*, or *fête champêtre*—the picnic, the season of our peace—already signifies the evolved sensibility: mature, reverential, an ability to step lightly, to smile, to love. These symbols are French and they are catholic, the very primeval relationships which evoke an ecological web, in whose biological nexus reclines the human tribe, graceful and inspired.

Chartres enshrines the longings and logic of such purity and cleanliness within ramparts extending more than 400 feet in depth. Coupled with its height and width, the structure must figure nearly half-a-million cubic feet of interior light. Of inner luminescence.

I stood in that confluence of cobalt, leaning lightly against the stone flanks, knowing that each stone, plastered with lime cement, reflected the touch of a forebearer.

In the space of a cathedral, any cathedral, time has been collected like water in an ancient cistern. Step into that vaulted stream of light, smell the gravely porous musk, the centuries-worth of candle and censer; attune yourself to psalms or the shuffling footsteps, the coolness which is of antiquity and modernity.

A cathedral such as Chartres has transcended its allegories and personages and the politics of creed that financed it, burned it down, rebuilt it, according to the whims of sovereigns and spiritual egos. But what has resulted atop that now touristy hill is a medieval miracle that corresponds to the potential for revelatory change in any one human personality, the minute he or she crosses its threshold, embarking on a journey of meditative sentience.

The cathedral is therapeutic, a palliative, a four dimensional aesthetic experience that approximates the heart's own ecosystem. Gothic construction allows one to enter the body, enter the world, to go inside all contradiction, hate, love, birth, death, and there, standing, sitting, whispering, to contemplate; to walk leisurely about its cloisters and re-attain one's balance.

It is the stepping inside which has enormous consequences in all other spheres. And Chartres is as good a place as any to revisit the phenomenon.

We step into the same river but once, said Heraclitus. The aphorism is annoying to anyone who favors the steadfast over growth; who is impatient with change and the everpresent possibility that the mirror we look into is bound, occasionally, to reflect the face of a stranger. Who is uncomfortable, in other words, with nature. The cathedral, itself a river, absorbs any and all discomfort. The businessman forgets his calculations. The tyrant kneels before the sacred relic, as Henry IV did dozens of times, right over there, beneath the roseate Apostles whose outstretched arms convey the blessings of sunrise and of late afternoon. The child and its parents step backward with their eyes fixed upwards, putting their hands into the light, touching it, holding on to it. Arguments lose their steam, agitation settles, the petty goals of earthly desire are, for a time, stifled by higher callings.

Chartres, for all of its man- and woman-made dimensions, is nothing more than stone and heated silicon and mineral paints, fitted in proportions which—like the river—are constantly in flow. The flow of light that has been invited in, to remain, century after century, and to shower each individual with his own reflection. The light of conscience. The light of hope. The light of privacy and endearment. For those moments, or hours, I am lacking for nothing. Filled with echoes, incense, motes mirroring motes, particles of the yin and the yang streaming towards the sublime creation itself, like angels ascending and descending the ladder to paradise, all around me, inside me. No consciousness, per se, only the perfect sensation of movement across continents. To circumambulate the Chartres Cathedral from within is to travel the extent of Africa, Asia, the polar regions, of the whole world, all in the topography of the inner soul. What does it mean? What can any revery mean? For how long can it remain potent? What good is it outside?

Outside, stepping into the glare, does the same life resume? Not after

Chartres, or not exactly. The secret code of the cathedral has hatched its own extenuating impulses, be they French, Italian or Tibetan. To sustain that inner light. That countryside which is so French. Nullify all those French nukes, guarantee their geese, safeguard their snail. But leave the French grape, tablecloth, the bread and olives alone. Practitioners of the picnic—an art form that spans Chartres and the salvation of the world in a single afternoon.

[1] Evagrius Ponticus, *Treatise on Prayer*, in Thomas Merton's *The Climate of Monastic Prayer*, p. 111, Irish University Press, 1969.
[2] Clarence J. Glacken, *Traces on the Rhodian Shore—Nature and Culture In Western Thought From Ancient Times To The End Of The Eighteenth Century*, pp. 321-339, University of California Press, Berkeley, 1967.
[3] ibid., p. 350.
[4] Gregory of Sinai, early 14th century, quoted in *Sinai*, by Heinz Skrobucha, translated by Geoffrey Hunt, p. 46, Oxford University Press, London, 1966.

XII
Mountain Meditation

Sevetha pantani senasanani
careyya samyojanavippamokkha
(Meaning: Seek lodgings distant from the haunts of men, Live there in
freedom from the bonds of sin.)

—Sampati[1]

In this mental journey—from southern Argentina to the heights of Tibet—I follow the universal prayer of high altitude; a guided visualization according to the tenets of Buddhist Abhidharma Triloka meditation. To be left ecstatically alone atop Mount Su-Meru, and then released in consciousness back down, among the living, at the edge of the glacier.

A few years ago, somewhere in the Cordillera Darwin along the Argentine/Chilean border, I found a mossy-like cloister of granite boulders, hardy beech trees, trickling water and luscious grasses on the side banks of a mountain. All around me were untrammelled glaciers descending toward the cobalt-glinting Straits of Magellan. In the distance, the eerily still whitecaps of the Drake Passage ruffled to and from oblivion. The coalescence of dramatic vistas and sharp angles, of a multivariety of plant life and ice, of rock and recurring storm, set me off balance, which is precisely where I wanted to be.

For many days I stayed in this place, alone, of an "innocent eye"—as some Impressionist painters described an aborginal confrontation—cultivating atunement with the way things possibly were, not just how they looked or felt. By seeking riff, abyss, cranny and crevass, I was placing myself in the confidence of the mountain, allowing for whatever turns, boredom, sleep, zeal or serendipity might befall me.

Within hours I found myself trudging up a glacier towards the nearest arête. And soon afterwards, I was swept by an avalanche which penetrated every pore of my body with dazzling cold. I managed to hold on to a rock (thus this reminiscence), continued my ignorant ascent, stayed a few pilgrim's moments on the summit for a superficial taste, then quickly descended the 80 degree, 1200 foot cliff in a Tierra del Fuegan downpour. By the time I had regained my nesting site amidst the lichen and moss, something warm and coaxing had begun to work its way into my introversion. A caesura in the storm, and an even more significant break in my normal train of thought. One might characterize it as a fairy tale, in which normally discreet elements began whispering; typically silent plants suddenly burst out in song. What was a creek was now a waterfall, its cavalcade leonine, its inner sluice of bottom-dwelling rocks cacophonic, as they rumbled along unseen at high megahertz. The checkered sun varied in temperature from second to second. A sun so powerful, so God-like, I dared not stare into its unmediated face even for a second. Nothing remained the same, the world's timing trans-formed into a tempest, a natural frenzy which denied me the contemplative hours I would have associated with an alpine meadow beneath the peak. But the meadow was no safe haven. Like the avalanche it roared all around me, alive with THINGS.

I took off all my clothes and lay about in the high grass, sensually aroused, mentally on fire. I was still damp with the aftermath of 10,000 tons of ice that had cascaded out in the air, right over me, through me, down the mountain wall into a perfect zen koan of whiteness, and now, cooling down, was myself a precipitate, a cloud over water, heat diffusing across surface area. A physical property called man.

Around me, a universe. Golden Polypody ferns, as smooth as silk, and flowering moss (*Pyxidanthera barbulata*), its rhizoid threads, germ cells and spore cases cleaving the granitic crevices, doting on every gentle incline, a wet garden of chlorophyll to the touch. On the rocks, other threads, woven into buds of algae and fungus (*Cladonia rangiferina*), rudiments of the earth's original soils. And there, two spectacular Morpho butterflies waltzing in the air. And something like a European stag beetle groping downslope, headed somewhere, beneath bunchberry and flowering almond, to its perfect heaven, its dark and leisurely hold in the roots of life, a family, a vague murmuring of ideas, a hot sauce of impulses.

I dig my fingers into the granular cogwheel ores of Bournonite which lace the soil, sulfides of lead and copper, antimony and arsenic. Felsite porphyry, intrusive igneous formations, andesite and diorite. The grasses are wild, the water like wine. Golden bees, fungus gnats and snow flies appear, then disappear.

Overhead, lenticular clouds mosaic the firmament. Striations of storm, patchwork furies of wind and climate. A dialogue of saints, parables of weather, universal phoneme—the language of animals, of plant and insect, crystal and mineral—gustily arranged in an on-going score of musical energy. Around me, messianic mountain wall. Fertile distances, views of the century.

What did I have that might add to such an orchestra?

I was empty. Emptied and emptying.

The reverie of immersion and discomfort escalated. My head against the pillow of slope, eyes lidded, ears frothing with the incoming sensorium, I must have lost consciousness for I was suddenly jettisoned and aloft, a particle physic in the greater rapture. Hours elapsed.

Eagle, ant, mist in my perceptionless perception; a clod of soil, a mite, a power unseen in the alpine amphitheatre of South America, where spindly legs and human arms, a head of stubborn bone and mind minus calculations, was borne by the wind into spheres of unknowing.

The way a certain phrase of music enters the confluence of one's soul, or a painting infiltrates the headwaters of the moment and becomes all of inner nature; like that I was the hundred-thousand songs of Milarepa, medieval Tibetan saint, poet, mystic, troubador; the mayfly, destiny played out in a matter of hours; the Antarctic gale, 110 knots, all day long, year after year, at Cape Dennison; or the aeolian winds atop Aconcagua, over 23,000 feet high, to the north. I was the ultramarine of Vermeer and the sullen harmonic convergence of Beethoven. The mad priapic antics of copulatory ladybugs on the rocks, and the winter tumult of off-shore swells in the straits.

I was the beginning and end of all natural scenery, to paraphrase John Ruskin. The point of convergence where every acuity, sensation, mindless instinct, all-embracing desire, atmospheric indistinctness, transport of phero-mones, increase of blood flow, riveted eye, bolting finger, upset equilibrium, agitated scent, fantastic tongue and terrified hope met head-on in the free space of the mountain air.

Grovelling. Wanting to be part of it. Incomplete. A yearling. First time out. Aposiopesis. Electrifying. Pre-linguistic, post-semantic. Deep structure psychosis. Back-to-nature boiling point. A fever to be re-born, in the making. Milestones scattering away like so much dross and spray.

Such that I was a drenched animal of ideas, no responsibility on this planet, to myself, to anybody else. Nothing to prevent my utter floating away. Which is precisely what happened, for hours, for days.

Lost? In space?

Precisely.

And the coming back down. Teeming with analogues and repercussions. Metaphors and a profusion of language that flows in like waters from a ruptured dam.

A bird—something like a Townsend's Solitaire—has just landed on my lap, demanding company or food. Chirping boisterously, the look of reincarnation in its crazed, ruffled eyes.

For a few brief moments, I had become something other than myself. I cannot say what it was, who I was, but I am convinced that it was something other, no identity, no "ego," no Michael Tobias.

A goner in nature. Transfixed. Purgatory. Floating. The stunning sense that death does not exist, or is nothing more than a good hot bath on a Sunday morning with a copy of the *New York Times* and a chocolate croissant in hand—a warm soaking in the tub of the Earth, perfectly luxurious.

Such moments are universally allotted to what is normally described as meditation. Animals of all kinds seem to partake of these special abstractions, whereby the organism, conventionally trained to survive, lets go, however briefly, and dozes in the worldly thrum of existence. I have witnessed Golden langurs in Bhutan contemplating the way the light in late afternoon played through a deodar stand and have read of a certain chimpanzee meditating before a waterfall in East Africa.[2] Anyone who has spent time around Koalas, penguins, parrots, dogs, cats, butterflies, otters, dolphins, in short—around living organisms—knows that the capacity for rapture is universal. It does not depend upon poets exclaiming the excellence of nature, nor theologians commending the supreme joy of the creation.

Obviously.

On the other hand, poets depend upon poets, theologians upon theologians, and the individual upon his own inner voice. Reaching that voice, I have found, is far more difficult than reaching the summit of a mountain. And this, I suppose, is why the literature and traditions of mountain people and mountain thinking is so deeply inward and rooted to spiritual yearning.

From the earliest times, mountains were sacred. The summit was already in the heavens. And the base of the mountain was attached to that summit so that all animal life could partake of something divine. And this early ecosystem of religious ordinance seems to have been a universal principle inherent to human aspiration and aesthetics.

The mountain is revered throughout the Bible, not just with reference to Mount Sinai, but to Zion, Nebo (where Moses died and was buried), Tabor,

Moriah, Peor, Mizpah, Gibeah, Ophrah, Ebal, Gerizim, Gilead, Carmel, Hermon, the Mount of Olives and Golgotha. How much of Western culture is encapsulated in these names, these vague sun-drenched outcrops of prehistory? I have climbed many of them, including the sheer 800 foot granite East Face of Sinai, above St. Catherine's Monastery in the Sinai Peninsula; and know that these are enchanted peaks, scattered with bones and mortars and pestles and Nabatean inscriptions; with fossilized goat turds and cactus spines and dung beetles. With pottery shards and footprints, apostolic ghosts and the torment of martyrs. Mountains alive with inner voices.

Other revelatory ensembles confront the pilgrim on every mountain in the world. The echos rise up like a Bach chorale or Acoma native's flute solo. Greek and Navajo shepherds, tinkling bells on the rams, purple velvet skirts on the women. Dust and the scent of ancient olive groves.

King Wu sacrifices to the spirits of Ho and the highest hills. Muhammad ascends on his horse beyond Qaf, the earthly mountain boundary, into heaven. The Egyptian Ra, Sun God, ascends on a ladder known as the Maquet, engraved on many of the tombs throughout the Old and Middle Kingdoms. *The Book of the Dead*, in both Tibetan and Egyptian, provides a map to heaven via the mountains. Bridges, spiral staircases, minarets, sacred rocks, ziggurats, gothic ceilings, ladders, pyramids, stupas, chhortens, cave ceilings, towers, pillars, all simulate the height and celestial aura which the mountain has imprinted in the human imagination, from the Koran to the Mahabharata. As Jorge Louis Borges has written in his "Utopia of a Tired

Man," though everywhere on earth all plains are one and the same, no two hills are alike.

It was this inner sanctum of religious weight, of those elements which universally commend the eye at a distance, from ground level to the idea of heaven, which prompted the 28th patriarch to succeed the Buddha, Bodhidharma, an Indian by birth, to come to China in 520 A.D. and there initiate what has come down to us as Zen. He did so by meditating wordlessly for nine years before a rock wall.

Such meditation clearly entered into the extraordinary efforts expended in the creation of pyramids and ziggurats. These cosmic mountains were the marriage of heaven and earth, where priest and priestess acted out the carnal re-creation of the world, fornicating in a rocky chamber a few hundred feet above the desert floor.

In Ethiopic, *dabr* means both mountain and monastery. The implicit fusion, a religious-physical relationship, is widespread. My mind reels with the abundant geography of mountain meditation: the mountain temples of Arunachaleshvara in southern India, Angkor Wat, Borobudur, that labyrinth of pre-Cortezian pyramids which Octavio Paz describes as always containing other pyramids under them: the Mayan Temple at Tikal in Guatamala, the Toltec Temple of Quetzalcoatl, the Temple of Kulkulcan, El Castillo at Chichen Itza in the Yucatan, the Honduran Acropolis of Copan, and the adobe Olmec structure at La Venta in Mexico (the earliest known artificial mountain in the American hemisphere, constructed about 800

B.C.). At Montserrat in Spain, at Mount Athos in Greece, in the village of Machu Picchu, the cagoulards of Cappadocia, even in the cliff dwellings of the American Southwest—whole lives, whole centuries, under the spell of the mountain wall.

The documents attesting to this historical passion for alpines and alpine gods are themselves a library of vast and varied directions. In the ancient Near East, in Greece and Rome, one is everywhere touched by Hittitean texts, royal seals, cartouches, friezes, pre-cuneiform pictographs, characters in classical Assyrian and hieroglyphic, steles, the metaphorical language of Homer, the lexicographical works of Apollodocus and Nicander, the poetry of Theocritus and Philostratus, the writings of Ovid, Horace, Propertius and Livy. By the vast panoply of Greek and Phrygian gods, Cybele foremost among them.

Mountain ascent figures prominently in the earliest Judaic and Christian literature—from the *Testament of Abraham* and the *Ascension of Isaiah*, to the *Ascent of Mount Carmel* by St. John of the Cross, the *Lucan* and *Johannine Resurrections* and the *Vita Antonii* by Athanasius. All of Western asceticism—and with it, the monastic ideal, the psychology of exile, of peregrinations, pilgrimage, and baptism in the wilderness, of the wilderness itself—is indebted to the mountain.

Mountain temples, where thought takes pause and the body its commerce with the gods, has utterly transformed the nature of religion in Asia. It has been said that the Kashmiri Himalaya, for example, have no space even the size of a sesame seed that is not a Hindu place of pilgrimage. To even gaze from afar upon the Himalayas, according to the Hindu, is to be cleansed of all sin. To actually drink of the Himalayan waters is to be instantly catapulted into paradise.

Concerning the Hindu and his mountains, Miguel Serrano has written, "This extraordinary people had created a mythology as gigantic as the mountaintops which surrounded their country. These very mountains were united to their souls...Like most people who look upon nature as something symbolic, they are forever condemned to the eternal and unmeasurable..."[3]

And it was precisely this intuitive grasp of an ungraspable universe that promises the Hindu, like the Buddhist, his mountain paradise, whether atop the Tibetan Su-Meru, the Japanese Fuji or the Chinese Omei-Shan.

Like the Gnostic ascetics of Sinai who stood atop towers awaiting revelations (Simone Stylites most celebrated among them), both Hindus and Buddhists, since ancient times, have also been accustomed to a psychological process whereby the initiate, the lover of high places, sought some form of transcendence on the mountain. Buddhist Abhiddharma Triloka philosophy gave a spatial meaning to the psyche, merging a Himalayan landscape of symbolic import, with all of the ultimate injunctions of Buddhist doctrine. The result is a series of meditations, best undertaken high on a mountain, or before an image of a mountain.

The path leads from the realm of the unfulfilled, of aggression and desire, of animal existence and sensual delight, to the realm of pure mentality, of pure form, and finally, to the summit of Mount Su-Meru (called by the Tibetans *Dise*, by the Hindu *Kailas* or *Kailasha*). The peak actually exists, at 22,028 feet, near the Indo-Western Tibetan border, and has been the site of intensive pilgrimage for at least 1200 years.[4]

Once on the summit, the realm of true meditation begins. Initially, it hinges upon the consideration of the infinity of space as the sole object of consciousness (*Akasanantyayatana*). Such consciousness, having begun in purity, atop a cold, windswept Tibetan desert peak, already comes recommended on the basis of a certain focus, uncluttered, whose only conceivable source of distraction is survival. But then, those who have reached Su-Meru's summit are said to have already gotten past such mundane concerns. Infinity, more or less available at a glance in any direction, has the purpose of reminding one's inner Being of its connectedness to the universe, its undifferentiation. But the reminders are meant to be inherent to the experience, without the need or want of explanation or elaboration.

Shortly thereafter, that consciousness itself becomes aware of the act of consciousness. It is a tautology played out until, from some deeper source before conscious mind, it is felt to be empty, like the infinity around it (*Vijnananantyayatana*). Awareness of emptiness is also awareness of paradox—for if it is empty, how can there be awareness? Realization craves lack of realization; but to know it is to undo what one has attempted to know. So that knowledge is stricken with mind-reversals, with the barriers and irresistable connections of subject and object. The paradox is known as *Akimcanyayatana* and is considered akin to the ultimate limit of perception (*Naivasamjnanasamjnayatana*), Sanskrit terms which are themselves, to a Westerner, hefty barriers. Beyond these conceptual Chinese boxes within boxes, is *arupa*, the absolute peace, *nirodha*, cessation, leading to *Nirvana*, death, ultimate tranquility.

In the whole history of religions, the Abhidharma summit meditation on Su-Meru is a uniquely refreshing attempt to incorporate the wilderness into the mind. To take the Earth literally; to confer upon the symbolic the physical, and vice versa.

Ancient Taoists considered the mountain fundamental to their own philosophy. The great master Yao was said to have spent much of his time naked on the ice in an attempt to communicate with mountain divinities. Those who mastered the meditation were immortal. In his Taoist treatise, *Pao-p'u-tzu*, Ko Hung (284-362) wrote, "All those cultivating the divine process go to the mountains...for all mountains...contain gods...proportional to the size of the mountain."

Writing of one of the early Taoist sacred mountains, T'ien t'ai, the ancient poet Sun Ch'o explained that, "Relaxed by discourse on what lies Beyond the Symbols...I yield to conversation's joys throughout the day, equivalent to utter silence in 'not speaking'...Once in view of the peak's Red Wall and Cascade, the mountain-climber is already within the realm of Taoist immortals."[5]

Later on, in the late Middle Ages of Japan, the Shugendo ascetics embarked upon even more radical forms of Abhidharma-like meditation, utilizing ropes to suspend themselves off cliffs (*suzukake*), where they then underwent other psychological ordeals. Climbing as an act of worship (*sangaku tobai*) and ascetic confinement in mountains (*sangaku rengyo*) are still practiced today in Japan and Korea by the Shugendo *yamabushi* (mountain priest) initiates. What does it all mean?

Mountain meditation in Asia took on countless forms, but all were congruent with the notion that the mountain was alive, a life that human beings should come to know, a space we should come to inhabit; that "mountains (themselves) meditate," a passage written in the sixth khanda of the *Chandogya Upanisad* and elaborated in felicitous detail by the 13th century Zen master Dogen, in the 29th book of his *Shobogenzo*, "The Mountains and Rivers Sutra."

But perhaps no other poet so evoked the spiritual mountain as the 8th century Chinese ascetic, Han Shan, a renegade monk and scholar-farmer who went off into the wilderness of T'ien t'ai, scribbled some 300 poems on bark, floated them down rivers, and eventually disappeared, having become legendary. He is said to have written, "Pondering these questions, I sit leaning against the cliff while the years go by, Till the green grass grows between my feet, And the red dust settles on my head, And the men of the world, thinking me dead, Come with offerings of wine and fruit to lay by my corpse."[6]

Like Near Easterners, Romans and Greeks, the Asian mind—fascinated by topography, blessed by high peaks all around and a penchant for symbolism—worshipped and merged with the alpines. The mountain pastoral paradise thus emerges—whether in the Renaissance or Hudson River School pictorial realms, in the early U.S. Geological Survey photographs of the American West, or in European Romantic literature, music and painting—as a supreme incentive, the philosophical and expeditionary point of departure for hundreds of millions of aspirants loyal to wild country.

The mountain exists inside the person, and, as such, provides an interior image or icon ready-made for meditation.

Begin at the bottom, the mind fully attuned. Start up the wild moraines, dip down onto the glacier, skirt the crevasses and continue upwards, from ledge to ledge, taking note of the spectacular airs, the distant calling of insects, the howl of the wind, the high-flying birds. The mountain ecosystem is part of the person. Enlightenment may take but moments, as in the Zen satori. Or it may take hours, months, even years. But eventually, one will reach a summit. From which, peering out into life, there is a whole new way to be; a new strength and vigor to support one's goals and convictions.

Having climbed the inner mountain of oneself, the outer wilderness will feel altogether familiar and comforting.

When people sometimes ask me why I climb mountains, the only thing I can think to say is, because I am a human being.

[1] Uttered by the ancient Brahma Sampati in *Milindapanho*, quoted in *Early Buddhist Monachism: 600 BC - 100 BC*, by Sukumar Dutt, p. 115, New York: Dutton & Co., 1924.

[2] Harold Bauer apparently observed a solitary chimp that trekked to a waterfall, evidently for the sheer pleasure of communing with it. Melvin Konner has compared this to the origin of human awe. In Konner's *The Tangled Wing: Biological Constraints in the Human Spirit*, New York: Holt, Rinehart & Winston, 1982.

[3] See Serrano's *The Serpent of Paradise: The Story of an Indian Pilgrimage*, 2nd. ed., translated by Frank MacShane, Harper & Row Publishers, New York, 1972.

[4] See T. S. Blakeney's article, "Kailas: A Holy Mountain," in *The Mountain Spirit*, edited by Michael Tobias and Harold Drasdo, London, Victor Gollancz Ltd., 1980. See also, Shri Bhagwan Hamsa, *The Holy Mountain - Being the Story of a Pilgrimage to Lake Manas and of Initiation on Mount Kailas in Tibet*, Faber and Faber, London, 1934.

[5] Translated by R. Mather, "The Mystical Ascent of the T'ien t'ai Mountains," *Monumenta Serica*, Vol. 20, pp. 226-245.

[6] Translated and edited by Burton Watson, *Cold Mountain Poems*, Columbia University Press, New York, 1972. See also, *The Mountain Spirit*, edited by Tobias and Drasdo, p.251, Victor Gollancz Ltd., London, 1980.

XIII
Visionary Landscapes

Rocks and waves and sky, which do not propagate their species—
to which, therefore, Natural Selection in Darwin's sense
cannot be applied—exhibit colour-schemes as remarkable
as those of animate Nature."

—from *The Revelation of God in Nature*[1]

Each of us paints our life, seizes a perspective, adopts a color scheme, a meaning, determines the horizon and goes there or not. Our visions arise in nature and speak to us night and day. If we open our eyes, and will embrace what we see—what is everywhere about us—life can be all we'd want it to be. This is my reading of certain individuals, like Leonardo da Vinci, Jan Vermeer and Nikos Kazantzakis, three men who meditated deeply.

Certain small objects, worn photographs, yellowed diary pages, patchworks and medleys in the attic, seem nearly to extend the grey matter out beyond its solar system of thought into a past as distant and unfathomable as far-off stars. Memories concentrated in a small way, an engraved wedding ring, a personal memento.

To my way of seeing and feeling, great paintings accomplish a similar, an even more concentrated journey. Their light has traveled through time, has addressed the eye and its many senses, linking one meditation to another. In the viewing space of a great painting, like minds share the recognition of human vulnerability, pleasure and conjecture.

A sense of indisputable beauty emerges in the magical moment of a painting; a history forms there in that tenuous space between the viewer and the canvas. It is a matter of inches or feet, connecting perspicuity, the aesthetics or adrenalin of desire, with solid realization. Though it is two-dimensionality addressing three-dimensional truth, in its very truncation, the humanity bursts from the frame, occupies a role in one's life, and leaves its mark like no other neural stimulus.

The visionary landscapes defy categorization. Leonardo da Vinci's "Ginevra de Benci" in the National Gallery in Washington is, quintessentially, a woman. To her lower right, however, is a tropical swamp. Columbus might have bushwacked through it; the first couple surely copulated there. The rear landscape, however diminutive, is a rich setting for Ginevra's portrait, a portrait of a portrait, a haiku within poetry. In fact, the rear window in Renaissance figurative works is key to understanding how several hundred years of social critique and cultural yearning actually operated. Today, we are the beneficiaries, having consciously subsumed the wilds, no longer so pointedly in rear windows, but all around us. The painters of the Renaissance who knew of this natural collision course are too numerous to delineate. But each of them quietly stationed their patron or virgin before the same beckoning, attenuated wilderness. Man and woman were certainly not the measure of all things, in these paradoxical icons of psychic investiture. "Ginevra" is a study in reciprocity, between viewer and viewed. Importunate in her poignant queries, she asks us to consider the nature of our own identities, which are ever enshrined in the unknowable landscape behind both of us. The painter, da Vinci, has acutely fashioned her solidity, conjuring a universal beauty that is only true because her poetry has been engulfed in the nature that encompasses her. Take away the tropical background and Ginevra loses her identity, vacillates for eternity without meaning. Her magnetism is dependent on the garden that blesses her beauty. The similitude is what speaks to me. It means everything. In his "Treatise on Painting," da Vinci had written, "In such walls (mountains, the wilderness) the same thing happens as in the sound of bells, in whose strokes you may find every word which you can imagine..."[2]

The painter seeks meaning. There are those who rightly argue that painting has nothing to do with meaning, per se, but with direct, unmediated existence. Conversely, others would insist that existence is not a matter of being, or non-being, but of semantics. These contentions, the endless possibilities, shed little light on what is actually happening in a landscape painting. Happening. For though the paint may seem static at a given moment, in actual fact its crackles, chemical reactions are continuing. Dust is accumulating. Grime is effecting the micro-fissures as sure as any crevasse in a glacier, which moves according to its own time. Light is emanating from within the greatest of the old masters, who knew how to trigger it and invested their multiple glazes with sometimes a dozen, or two dozen separate chemical premonitions. The painting is moving, alright, and the attuned soul catches this phenomenon.

To meditate upon a painting—it doesn't matter where it rests—is to be entranced not once, but twice, by nature; to engender the same metaphors of distance and immersion, proximity and horizon line, that captivated not only the artist, but the landscape itself.

What do I mean by that? Anthropologist Colin Turnbull described the Ik (Kwarikik) of East Africa, a tribe that would not be the Ik if not for the mountain on which they lived (Mount Morungole in northern Uganda), and conversely, a mountain that would not be a mountain if not for the Ik. So the landscape has its own varied psychic and biological reciprocity with every painter. Their relationship is alive, evolving, like the oils and vegetables and minerals that populate and catapult the hazy retinal eidolons, after-echoes, lingering images and dreams, into solid form.

The painter is the viewer is the painter. And each is part of the landscape. The viewer stands admiringly in the space, the nature of the painting, as the painter himself was engulfed in the scene to which his powers of feeling and observation and being ascribed. The equation is all art. Whether, as with Turner, the landscape was usually accomplished in a London brick atelier, or, with John Ruskin, out along the trails of Fontainebleau and Venice and Chamonix.

Kuo Hsi, the Sung Dynasty painter and critic had described in his own "Essay On Landscape Painting" how the painter must place himself within the mental/physical landscape, donning a rucksack, spending the night at a bivouac in the foreground, and continuing into the middle ground of mists, towards the base of the high peaks. Once there, on the second or third day, the painter begins his ascent into the higher reaches. He fords rambling brooks, scrapes and gathers his way up moss-slimy brant, and there realizes the point of his possible disappearance. The process occurs slowly or quickly. Ruskin believed that the intensity of a kinesthetic experience can last no longer than 45 seconds (the power of sensation when peeling an orange, for example).

Most poetic meter does not exceed three seconds. But Kuo Hsi gave it far more time, convinced that aesthetic jubilation was no one-liner, no Zen belly laugh, but rather a sustained communion that enabled different species to communicate, and which granted matter to mind, and mind to matter.

In speaking of mountains to his son, Kuo Hsi wrote, "Inexhaustible is their mystery. In order to grasp their creations one must love them utterly, study their essential spirit diligently, and never cease contemplating them and wandering among them."[3]

This is clearly the sense of nature one obtains in Pure Land Buddhist painting. Pure Land is a branch of Mahayana that recognizes the Buddha Amitabha and his Western paradise (*saiho jodo*). Founded by the monk Honen during the 12th century in Japan, one of its three principle texts, the *Kammuryoju-ko (Sutra on the Meditation of the Buddha of Infinite Life)* treats of the psychic steps by which one may be brought to heaven. Collectively, those many steps are known as *henso*, visions of paradise. Like the Ladder to Paradise of St. John Climacus, composed in the early Middle Ages at St. Catherine's Monastery beneath Mount Sinai, or, in the manner of Buddhist Abhidharma Triloka mountain meditation, the journey is a psychological one which leads the practitioner into a mental landscape. He paints an image for himself of the perfumed waterfalls, the gem trees made of gold and crystal, the fruits and lotus lakes and angelic singers. *Henso* literally means "transformed configuration(s)," "visual transformations."[4] The meditator-as-landscape visionary, iconographer, voyager into picture, provides an exquisite technique for appreciating and re-creating great art.

To "get it" one has to go there in body or in spirit. And the effort can be extraordinary. Consider a hanging scroll entitled "The Mandala of Mount Potalaka," on the back wall of a shrine housing the Thousand-armed Kannon in the Senju-do of the Kaidan-in at Todai-ji in Nara, Japan. Potalaka, somewhere in the southern seas, was considered by Pure Land Buddhists to be the Bodhisattva Kannon's paradise on earth. (It is worth noting that *all* Pure Land Gardens of Eden are earthly ones, meaning that the meditation can result in real transformation. There is the outstanding promise of real cascades, real cherry blossoms, real stars at night.) The mountain paradise hosts a mesmerizing vertical world of perfectly austere tea houses, a palace, gates, curving bridges, monks journeying up along the labyrinth of gentle streams and luscious waterfalls. Willows are gold against the mauve streams and bristling whitecaps. The blues are grey and azure, the Earth becoming mist, the streams becoming veins, thinking curly-cues. Dragons and mythic four-legged creatures inhabit this absolutely exquisite universe which has managed to combine real architectural relics, courtyards, white sliding bamboo panels, and slate roofs with the Medieval Other World. The trees are touched with life. The effect is sensational. A combination Mustique and Bhutan. Kyoto's Ginkaku-ji shogunate garden palace, and Bora Bora. The eye lingers, transformed into loving pilgrimage.[5]

The landscape is fixed in the human ideal of it. This is an organic fact. An anology comes to mind. Jane and I recently cared for a baby blue jay, after it had been released back into the wild following a slight injury. For weeks it kept coming to our window for handouts. One day, I noticed it staring intently at other young blue jays converging in the late afternoon around our various feeders. I could see that the bird was staring contemplatively at the others, coming to terms I imagine with the fact that it, too, was a bird, designed to fly, to exhibit flocking behavior, to mate with another bird. To eat seeds, rather than microwaved white corn. This coming of age was embryological for the bird, an eternal return, the arrival at a place which he recognized at long last. It was incredible to behold.

The art of landscape, widely undefinable, performs a similar chime of recognition. We invented landscape, miniatures, intimations in the palm of a hand, mandalas and mantras, for a biological reason. Every landscape invokes a memory of that primordium of experience, a residual psychology of place. Place is the beginning and end of human awareness. Our birth, the span of our lives and our reincarnation, are about place. Many will argue that place is incidental. Where we just happen to be, with no consequence in terms of action, behavior, causation or moral plot line. All that is true with regard to circumstance, though even the vagaries may have their own karma. But the psychology of place is altogether different, encompassing inexplicable affinities, topophilia, innate disposition for color and obscurity. It refers to volition, reveries, fantasy, where we'd like to be. In sum, the landscape evokes an historical déjà vu. We've been there before. It is commensurate with our self-consciousness. Inarticulate longings on the part of the millions of visitors to the "Mona Lisa" relive the alter-ego of da Vinci's own personality and expeditions. Pilgrims to the Louvre have walked hundreds of feet to reach the painting. One is reminded of the initiates at Lascaux who crawled hundreds of feet through dark tunnels to attain the inner sanctum and there, by torch-light, view the spectacle of stag and bison migrating across the receding glacial backcountry of southwestern Europe and human pre-history. Upper Paleo-lithic viewers of the Lascaux frescoes must have recognized something of their own faint ontology and exodus, a genesis of feeling that had mysteri-ously survived in the darkness of Mother Earth.

In today's Paris, other initiates, whole families guided by curiosity and the light of the imagination, pay homage to da Vinci and are—if you've ever noticed—as taken with Mona Lisa as a blue jay with another blue jay. Remembrance of places past.

Da Vinci's *art* of landscape pilgrimage has entranced us. In the case of "Mona Lisa," as in "The Virgin and Child with St Anne," the landscapes, as recorded in the painter's Leicester notebook, point to the Alps, and to the region near Lake Maggiore.[6]

At the Bhutanese monastery of Paro Dzong, there is an alfresco mandala, an abstract expressionist landscape, entitled "The Mystic Spiral." A series of brightly painted concentric ellipses and asymptotes, overlaid spheres and ovals. It is meant to draw the viewer into a profound meditation on the limits of reason; to unleash the energies of nature in the psyche. To transcend the paradoxical entrapment of cause and effect, of language and expectation, of metaphor itself. To bring the transfixed gaze back to the original moment of appreciation and clarity that continues to characterize all other life forms, but has been obscured in the human animal.

Another clue to our salvation and permanent joy: "He was the greatest, the most lofty, the most permanent.. the most original genius of his age.... He has compassed the Infinite itself with mathematical precision....Alone and guideless, he has penetrated the remote caverns of the past and gazed on the primeval shapes of the gone world." That was part of E. Bulwer Lytton's eulogy to John Martin, whose modest little painting, "Sadak In Search Of The Waters Of Oblivion" can be found at the Southampton City Art Museum. The nobleman Sadak is portrayed climbing an impossible mountain of overhanging, incandescent glaciers, to the place where the djinn Alfakin had suggested the immortal lakes might be. At the time of its creation in 1812, the 23-year-old Martin had never ventured out of London, had never seen a mountain. And this was his first painting, one of the most remarkable of the whole Romantic era.

No reading of the period could have provided him such precise geological data. Nor such a grasp of perspective and proportion. What was it—some prefiguring incident in his life? The sight of the hundred foot cliffs outside of London? A reading of Milton? A dream? He had been a glass blower's apprentice; one of his brothers had burned down a building of parliament and been committed; another wandered the streets of London banging an Oriental gong around his neck, exclaiming, "I am William Martin, Philosophical conqueror of nations." A third brother committed suicide.

We have no way of knowing what it was that prompted Martin's five mile high Himalayas, his titantic figure struggling over a mantle shelf, naked, like Kazantzakis' Odysseus, grappling with the Beyond. The painting was viewed by Percy Shelley at the British Institution the year after it was painted.

Shelley devoted innumerable poems to the same theme, most remarkably in his alluring, inaccessible "Mont Blanc," a work of astounding contemplation whose imagery was meant to lead the reader, the viewer, into the wilderness of the mind.

The treasure map leads us onward; The search for those waters of oblivion, further and further…to the Hague, where there is an oil painting in the Mauritshuis museum by Jan Vermeer which conveys more of that clarity, that insight into human landscape, than perhaps any other creation. "View of Delft," painted around 1660, is nearly four feet wide and over three feet high. I have stood to the south of Delft, where Vermeer painted the landscape, looking towards the Schiedam and Rotterdam gates along the Schie River where barges once plied their trade. Where clusters of cloud, pungent with a local moisture that is uniquely and unexplainably Dutch, rise up in fantastically dispersed hues above the 400-year-old tilting red brick facades. This Holland of Vermeer's cannot, as Kenneth Clark suggested, be likened to any photograph, though for sheer acuity the comparison is intriguing. But unlike a photograph—the byproduct of a second or less, of mechanical and electronic means, a push of a button, the whimsy of a random eye, no matter how much one wishes to dignify the artist behind the instant—Vermeer's painting is the plodding outgrowth of possibly two years of intensive meditation. And Vermeer was a genius who cannot be figured out; our love for him is perfectly, purely, unrequited.

We are left to our own being, weeping and stranded in the appreciation, awestruck by his achievement, inconsolably pacing the void which is illumined only by his remains. His "View of Delft," like the majority of his other thirty-five known pieces, is like that rare South African black mineral, of which only three specimens have ever been found; or the equally scarce Martian meteorites recovered in the Antarctic. As durable as the cosmos; as frail as the snow flea which dies instantly in the palm of one's hand from the heat of warm-blooded curiosity.

The artist has completely altered the grading curve, if you will, of humanity. That such a man ever lived, in heroic silence, in deep and passionate love with Catharina, his wife; supported by Maria Thins, his mother-in-law; 43 when he suddenly died of a heart attack, leaving 11 hungry children; compels the heart to probe into every pointillist disc of brilliant color, to follow the thinking and feeling that went into the creation of "View of Delft." It is an astonishing painting. No one can be prepared for it.

At the lovely Mauritshuis, another painting by Vermeer, of his daughter, Maria, figured as an Orientalist erotic face, trembling and all-powerful, with a pearl earring and a blue and yellow turban, stares radiantly and forever across the room toward Vermeer's landscape, not thirty feet away. To one seated in the middle of the room, the cross-fire of these two spectacles, is like some psychic avalanche, force fields of human immortality as palpable as tidal waves. I have lingered there many days, my face into the wind.

Obsession has led many to unearth every possible fact of Vermeer's brief life. He wrote nothing. Until 1886, virtually no one else had written more than a line or two about him. When French journalist W. Thoré-Bürger published his monograph on the artist in the *Gazette des Beaux-Arts*, after having spent a decade combing every library, private collection, gallery, auction house and rummage sale across Europe, it was a monumental discovery, as important as Mendelssohn-Bartholdy's revival of J. S. Bach.

But the obsession leads, ultimately, to a day along the canals of Delft, to the Oude Langendijck at the corner of the Molenpoort, adjoining the St. Joseph Catholic Church, where Vermeer and Catharina lived. The house is gone. The surroundings have been overrun by exotic restaurants and tour buses. The kingfishers, grebes, herons and mallards remain along the polluted canals, feeding on the algae which festers in the pickerelweed. Still, Vermeer lingers in the air. One cannot feel enough about him. His paintings, spread out in at least seven countries, have become national pilgrimage points for hundreds of millions of people. They are, like the "Mona Lisa," wilderness areas unto themselves, gently against walls, the kind the Bodhidharma meditated before.

It is this topographical revelation, whether in the face of a girl, or the creases of a map in the "Artist In His Studio" (also known as "The

Allegory Of Painting") at the Kunsthistorisches Museum in Vienna, that marks Vermeer's spellbinding achievement; to have internalized nature to the extent of making posterity see, in the human being, the whole world, and thus, of completing the metaphor of mind in nature by self-inference, in color, tonality, form, pulse and desire. Vermeer embodies the act of transcendence and genetically imparts its technique and rationale to all who view and cherish his works.

This is what the visionary landscapes can accomplish: this vivid reminder that there is salvation in this world of a kind that is inherent to the beauty of the very planet we inhabit. By celebrating and revering the miracle of life, by personalizing the great principles of biology and physics and chemistry, we are taking evolution into the realm of aesthetics. Once accomplished, every other solution falls into place.

The joy of art, born of experience and meditation, of affirmation rather than rejection, guarantees a sound rebuttal to every nightmare.

I've often imagined a Vermeer in the arms of an emaciated sub-Saharan refugee; an exquisitely perfected 17th-century Delftian canvas of greys and ultramarines, of a woman by a window, sun pouring in from the south through the leisurely, brick-scented wilds of golden Delft; lying out on the cracked alkaline flats of Mali or Burkina Faso, the sun burning into the desolation on all horizons. You cannot drink Vermeer. Beside it, I see the bleached bones of dead cattle. I hear the soft sobbing of mothers for their ruined children. What then, one is led to ask, is the worth of such a painting, in a land at a time when one would willingly trade it for a glass of water? The life of a child?

The question is unanswerable. No contradiction can be contradicted. Multiply any number times zero and the entire edifice is swept up in the void. Or, as Gandhi so rightly stated, an eye for an eye and the whole world goes blind. Emptiness, evil, pain, are a contagion that cannot be forgotten, or shaken. Neither da Vinci nor Vermeer—nor every landscape in between—can solve a problem. They simply combat it by incremental change within the soul; providing a means for individuals who are interested to investigate the inner world, to be slowly invigorated, inspired, driven to obsession, as I have been.

The painter solves technical problems, to be sure. Vermeer unleashed Newtonian physics and the microscopic investigations of his friend van Leeuwenhoek in seeing the effect of light on a wall, upon a woman's face or a river, as if for the first time in Europe. Kuo Hsi deduced the subtle aspects of intimation, almost by way of some abstruse mathematical calculation, all in a mist-covered mountain, and then fathomed how to get there. Van Gogh's olive groves converted image into sense, starry nights and swirling fields into hunger; he learned how to ravish the eye; Victor Higgins' New Mexico provides a whole new revisionist history of the West shaped by color and invigorating cloud, by Native American sensibility and perspectives that are fresh and uncluttered. From Simone Martini's madonnas, Giorgione's "Pastorale," and John Martin's mountain otherworld, to Gustave Klimt's more familiar Austrian beeches, poppies and "Island in the Attersee," the landscapes of the mind have touched off new sciences. What did not exist has come to exist as surely as a newborn infant in the cracked deserts of the Sahel.

The painter does not salvage the world as it is. We know that. But by giving birth in his own right to positive energy, he manifests the creative possibilities in a world that knows no bounds.

It was this surpassing theory of creation which galvanized the work of one of this century's most exciting artists, the Greek poet, philosopher and novelist Nikos Kazantzakis. Zorba, St. Francis, Buddha, Don Quixote, Odysseus, Lenin, Moses, Christ…these were some of his own obsessions. Out of Kazantzakis' many journeys around the world and more than fifty books arose a transcendental method for discovering that joy in life, that Vermeer, which is possible, in spite of unrelenting tragedy.

In his remarkable little book, *The Saviors of God—Spiritual Exercises*, beautifully rendered by poet and translator Kimon Friar[7], Kazantzakis proposed an expedition into the landscape which, by his reckoning, would transport the individual right smack into the heart of cosmic, unknowable evolution. He described the odyssey in the following terms:

> An individual's first duty is to self-discipline and clarity.
>
> He then must reject all boundaries. As Lenin said, we must become as radical as the Earth itself.
>
> Having renounced the narrow, the limited, seeing life as with the

eyes of an eagle, the journeyer's third duty is to free himself from both mind and heart, to declare that nothing really exists, which is tantamount, of course, to admitting that EVERYTHING exists!

Kazantzakis then envisioned the great march: Beyond ego, beyond race, beyond mankind, beyond even the Earth.

His vision of these transformations involved three enduring relationships: people to people; people to god; people to Nature.

In the end, having reached beyond relationships, squared off with oneself, Kazantzakis formulated a profound silence, which—remarkably—he also declared does not exist.

Many have found in his works a testament to nihilism, which logically follows from his emphatic resistance to the paramount substance which so inheres, for example, in the painters I have described above. But I see in Kazantzakis the eternal striving itself, purified and freed from the shackles of conformity to such substance. A painter of images, nonetheless, but arrayed in an ethereal effort, words and stories, yearnings woven of a distant imagination that spanned a lifetime. His creatures—Zorba dancing on the beach, Odysseus climbing the iceberg, St. Francis taking off his clothes, Christ re-living his youth—have managed deftly to consolidate the greatest myths into a clear stream of consciousness. It relates to a stratum of experience that cannot be diminished. It does not exist only to the extent that it transcends mere existence.

This is the puzzle unburdened: Kazantzakis found a personal path that nurtured him, even during such horrors as the Nazi occupation of Greece, when for months all he had for nourishment was one spoonful of olive oil a day. He was so weak he could not lift himself from the bed in his home on the Island of Aegina, where he and his mate, Eleni Samiou, weathered the war. And it was during this period of extreme privation that Kazantzakis, in six weeks' time, wrote his novel, *Zorba the Greek*. It was his daily meditation—his imagination—that kept him alive, no matter how hard the Germans tried to do away with him.

On his windy gravestone above the Cretan town of Heraklion are written the words:

I fear nothing, I hope for nothing, I am free...

---

[1]*The Revelation of God in Nature* - a discussion between the Chaplain to H. M. the King, Rev. C. J. Shebbeare, and Joseph McCabe, author of "A Biographical Dictionary of Modern Rationalists, p. 35, G. P. Putnam's Sons, New York, 1924.

[2]Kenneth Clark, *Landscape Into Art*, p. 90, New York: Harper & Row Publishers, 1979.

[3]See Esther Jacobson Leong, "Place and Passage in Chinese Arts: Visual Images and Poetic Analogues," *Critical Inquiry* 3, no.2 (Winter 1976): pp. 345-68.

[4]See Joji Okazaki's *Pure Land Buddhist Painting*, p. 29, translated and adapted by Elizabeth ten Grotenhuis, Kodansha International Ltd., and Shibundo, 1977.

[5]ibid., pp. 76-77.

[6]op. cit., Kenneth Clark, p. 92.

[7]Simon & Schuster, New York, 1960.

XIV
Practical Immortality

This I tell you, Bhikkhus. Decay is inherent in all conditioned things.
Work out your own salvation, with diligence.

—Buddha's last words[1]

As biological beings propelled by an undefinable spark, it is not what we have accomplished that matters, but what we have dreamt. The dream of love. The dream of reason. The muses with whom we mutter sweet nothings. The planet recycles everything. Nothing is lost. Ever. Not even the spark which I know to be my true being.

Every prophet of any durability has tapped into the human yearning for immortality. At the same time, every map of even marginal interest has ordained a wild and inaccessible place for paradise somewhere in its maze of latitudes and longitudes. During the Renaissance, the precise whereabouts of paradise were argued and scrutinized. Explorers brought back fabulous legends (Marco Polo most extravagantly) which seemed only to confirm previous Biblical and prophetic assumptions regarding the Garden of Eden. That heavenly abode was believed to exist atop the Himalayas, a mountain range at times confused with Abyssinia, with India, even with the Caucasus. The confusion was irrelevant.

Journeys to paradise, in history, fable, romance, as in reality, were physical and this fact, this expeditionary adrenalin neatly counterbalanced the apothegmatic injunctions of the many holy men, Messiahs, apostles and visionaries throughout time who urged inward, rather than outward journeys.

Sri Krishna, for example, recommended to his disciples that they Get Wisdom; Buddha cautioned his friends to Forsake Desire; Christ encouraged Love and Charity; Lord Zoroaster stated emphatically, "Make Thyself

Pure;" Mohammed decreed, "Seek God." It was all the same thing. Cautions and advice meant to fulfill this life and guarantee the next.

Outward or inward, they are grand blueprints, larger than mere ideas; schemes that harbor no recognizable itinerary. And yet saints and adventurers, missionaries and gods, were usually real men and women who travelled, who related to nature in ways that catapulted their doctrines, served them as metaphor, and even added to the appeal of their transcendent messages. Indeed, each of them revealed their insight from hilltops, from gardens, from caves, or in stands of ancient forest. The great Taoist poet, Lao-Tzu, disappeared at the end of his life riding a bullock cart into the high mountains. Milarepa, Tibet's medieval prophet, spent his life climbing mountains and praising Buddha from high aeries in the snow. His biographer compiled Milarepa's exhausting saga from the slopes of Mount Chomolungma (Everest). Mahavira journeyed barefoot back and forth across India for forty years. Moses spent his own forty years wandering throughout Sinai, climbing mountains, talking with God. Christ went out into the desert, possibly even to Asia. The earliest Christian saints were all weather-hardened in Egyptian deserts like Chalcis, Scete and the Thebaid. Whether one speaks of St. Francis, Gregory the Great, Marpa, Padmasambhava, the countless guiding lights of every major religion or most of the philosophers, poets, and artists, there is a journey to be deciphered, often fraught with obstacles and transfiguring ascension.

Does this imply that tourism, however one labels it—adventure travel, exile, expatriotism, a passion for open spaces, peregrinations *ad terram sanctum*—is fundamental to the success of the soul, however one cares to paraphrase it?

No.

For the flamboyant aesthete of nature, the physical jubilators, any encumbrance of body, of free movement in the out-of-doors, must pose a terrifying challenge to an otherwise uncomplicated analysis of human experience. But what, then, does it mean to be born into captivity, to languish in a jail cell or under an oxygen tent, and to stay there one's whole life? Is not the imagination an expression of a soul which lives unfettered by the unpredictable vagaries of the body? Is not creativity in thought, rather than in deed, the basis of our salvation? Life itself, even brain-dead life, is a sacrosanct joy that legal debates and medical ethics will never know. Or are these just words, generous but futile queries to make the wonderment of life, of ecstasy and art and reincarnation, democratic? An equal opportunity theory of tragedy and Self?

Great art, brilliant poetry, massive erudition, insights into the distant universe, philosophical genius, abundant lives, have been kindled in bed, from a wheel-chair, or merely seated at a window staring out or staring in. It is easy to take a taxi to the airport. But you cannot take a taxi into your Self; there are no special passes available for weekend sojourns into the depths of one's subconsciousness. No front row seats overlooking the psyche. If anything, the human spirit is compelled into ever more glorious inward heights as the Nature which most people take for granted is denied us. This is why St. Augustine, in his *Confessions*, cautioned against too exhuberant an embrace of the mountain.

The ability to journey, to enjoy the natural world must be received as an additional blessing; the slightest scent of a flower an awesome gift; the vision of a Rufus hummingbird hovering over a dewdrop, or a Western Tanager against the twilight, among the greatest sights on Earth. I cannot comment intelligently or usefully, or begin to put myself in the place of a congenitally blind, deaf or crippled being. But we are all essentially bed-ridden souls. Not just in the literal sense that approximately one-third of our existence (thirty years out of a ninety-year old individual's life) is spent asleep. We are born, and usually die in bed. But in the fuller sphere of our inner life, which remains stilled in the private solitude of a name, a genetic heritage, a one-time personage. This cluster of privacy is like dried tinder, silent, motionless, ready to be ignited. Such is this tradition of solitude, be it monastic, ascetic or poetic—the origin of our thought, our inspiration and love affairs, of every aspiration and social commingling. This is the true environment of all human, animal and plant life; every rock on every mountain; every cloud in the sky; every wave and dust mote and sunbeam comes into this world and leaves this world, alone. *Monos pros monon*: alone with the Alone.

"What I have is my burning heart," wrote Wen T'ien-hsiang, the late 13th century Prime Minister who found himself a doomed prisoner. "It is as clean as blue sky which I see above. I am overwhelmed with grief. Cannot heaven come to my rescue? The old sages are far from me, but their pattern has remained before me for ages. When I read books near the window, the old tradition shines upon me like a picture."[2] Boethius, too, wrote his greatest work (*The Consolation of Philosophy*) from a jail cell, as did Cervantes his *Don Quixote*. There are countless examples of art and faith that prospered in confinement—the Blakelocks and Noldes—in tenements and poverty, in sedentary pain, without a blade of grass to be seen, fresh air to be enjoyed or the hope of physical or mental freedom to be savored.

Buddhist meditation begins in this aloneness, aware that millions of years of evolution have resulted in consciousness, the environment of the mind, with its own profusion of images, linked to other proliferating icons and desires, and so on *ad infinitum*. All the continents, local phenomena, dragons and stormy seas exist in the nervous impulses which animate the individual who has not necessarily taken a single step beyond his or her front porch. And what this suggests is that we can truly go anywhere in our minds, accomplish anything, realize peace, tranquility, purity, by nothing more exacting than contemplation. The inner life has no formal roadblocks, only obstacles of inclination.

Over a period of nearly two years, I spent time in Asian monasteries reflecting on the possibilities of this inner life at extraordinarily beautiful temples and ascetic cloisters.

At Palitana, Jaisalmer and Mount Abu, Jain bastions in western India, the intricate marble carvings and cool airs fill the spirit with a profound respect for animals, for the symbolic power animals have in our caudal memory. What quiet Jain reflection achieves is the animal in each of us. The Jain temple serves as an entranceway, a blessingway, an architectural ecology, of sorts, which coddles and solicits that vulnerable organism, the mind. The point of the Jain temples and of the pilgrimage to get there, is to reconnect with something wild that is in oneself.

At Thyangboche in Nepal, beneath Kantega and Tamserku, Ama Dablam, Nuptse and Chomolungma—mountains whose beauty and significance quickly escalate into the mental interior, where they remain forever—I was made aware that the highest mountain means nothing. Chomolungma is over 29,000 feet. Mt. Sinai, 8,000 feet, and a rock which I frequently climb above the ocean a mere twenty-five feet. Each of these holds for me the same key to the indoors. Thyangboche enshrines that truth.

So does Taktsang, situated spectacularly upon a 1500 foot granite cliff above Bhutan's Paro Valley. It was there that the great Tibetan wanderer and holy man, Dorje Trolo, decided to spend his life in meditation, perched upon that perilous ledge. What is the alluring chemistry of altitude that so induces the inner view, when—ironically—an alpine panorama seems more likely to overwhelm all introspection? I met a disciple of Trolo, worn down, radiant, emaciated, an ascetic who had lived most of his life at Taktsang. He was old, clad in a tattered red cape, barefoot and smiling; a ragamuffin remnant of human flesh who had achieved something remarkable by his persistence of inner vision. Out of the corner of his eye were reflected the surrounding mountains. But his focus was largely absorbed with an internal cosmology far more compelling.

In Ladakh, at Hemis, Thikse, Spituk, Phyang, Mulbeck and Alchi, monasteries situated above 11,000 feet, other puzzles of altitude revealed themselves in the guise of the Tibetan mantras, calculated to vibrate the chakras, the inner nerves, to awaken compassion, to spread mercy throughout the world, and to expedite the monks' passage from distraction and desire into the realm of unity and emptiness. Here were hundreds of monks, and a few nuns, spinning their *mani-chhos-khors*, metal cylinders filled with scraps of prayer, absorbed in the mesmerizing vocables, "Om Mani Padmi Hum," part of the Buddhist *Dhammapada* and *Tripitaka* canons, which they recited for up to six hours every day; a baritone chorale accompanied by drums and horns fashioned of human thighbone; by a tingling percussion that ricochetted through abbatial glows and dingy teak halls, off granite boulders and mountain walls. In Ladakhi, the translation reads, "I invoke the path of truth and the experience of universality so that the jeweline luminosity of immortal mind be unfolded within the depths of lotus-centered consciousness and I be wafted by the ecstacy of breaking through all bonds and horizons."

In Kyoto, atop Mount Hiei overlooking Lake Biwa, the whole of the forest, with its dozens of Shingon, Shinto and Tendai monasteries, commands an inner voyage. Nature and spirituality have quietly merged beneath the mottled cryptomeria glens. Of what does this "inner voyage" consist? For the Zen master, Dogen, author of the famed *Mountains and*

Rivers Sutra, nature was the inner eye, the enlightenment of reverse vision and reverse calculation. What does it mean? The natural world, in other words, was merely a reflection of the inner world: the more one saw, the more one recognized. This recognition started inwardly and was thus a mirror that enabled a person to stare directly into his own soul; to embark upon a dialogue wherein all the conventional rules of physics and cosmology, of biology and behavior were turned inside out. Blue mountains drifted across water. Shadows yielded detail, detail shadows. In every jolt, accompanying each thrust, was the stillness of inner existence, true Zen nature. Nature alone was capable of unleashing nature. Being brought Becoming into Being, as paradox upon paradox penetrated to the core, releasing the Self.

And even this Self, said Dogen, is perceived, finally, to rest upon the idea of Self—yet another paradox.

To listen to oneself recite the indwelling, or dwell on the imponderable, the poetic cancellation of opposites, is to have plunged into a never-neverland of unformed language, person, potential; where the new birth of a possibility—lodged in some timeless, immortal crevice—has its beginning. It is like an instinct newly discovered; a lost world of humanity attained in the most distant, untapped region of the self. In certain respects it must echo Keats' beguiling utterance, "My mind is a monastery," in which all of Romanticism and Modernism has been schooled.

All is relaxed. There is no sense that all these paradoxes-within-paradoxes are driving anyone particularly insane, though the trappings and expectations of ascetic life are not particularly charmed or favorable. At Ryoan-ji, where the stones have been resting in the sand for centuries, there is no pressure to "find" anything; the unleashing is timeless; day by day, ever inwardly, as the true nature of Self emerges, tenderly, eyes and ears eavesdropping on the void, goals slipping away as the river of one's discipline—inaudible, nonsensical, anonymous—carries the life we would call our own toward a place where we've never been. Or have we? The place of true nature.

Is it good, is it useful, is it beautiful? These questions are no longer relevant to the explorer of inner being.

An interesting measure of that renunciation was always to be found in the forbidding desert of Sinai, engulfing St. Catherine's Monastery, where I once lived for months in a lovely little cave.

There, the dozen or so Greek Orthodox monks spoke of a certain bliss accomplished by the daily fusion of ascent and inner meditation. Fifteen hundred years ago, the biographer of St. Anthony described how the ascetic frequently reached the height of his contemplations at the very moment that he had attained the summit of Mount Sinai, and that this was no coincidence. The emphasis was always on the inner, Platonic world, the world of forms, which reflected the outer universe.

John Muir, after several years roaming the High Sierra, the North Cascades and Southeastern Alaska, came to very much the same unison of inward ardor and outward homage. The homage is pleasurable, but not essential. And he termed this equation, or method "practical immortality."

It is indeed an ancient technique for mastering not only mountains, but oneself; a universal method by which nature meditation—be it Taoist, Essene, Gnostic, Greek Orthodox, Tibetan, Jain, Sherpa, Zen, Shinto or Talmudic—achieves biological integrity that surpasses the human concept of enlightenment.

But what does it mean, exactly? What can there be beyond enlightenment?

The beginning of the world. A quality of experience which cannot be articulated; that transcends a roof over one's head, creature comforts, the ego, even life and death.

"I learned not to fear infinity," wrote the poet Theodore Roethke. "The far field, the windy cliffs of forever, the dying of time in the white light of tomorrow..." [3] Practical immortality is not going to reduce the deficit or feed hungry Africans. It's personal; it's neither mental nor symbolic. What words one uses to hint at it are necessarily stuck in a deep and distracted mire that comes not even close to intimating it. But even from afar, a koan of recognition, a vague sense of it remains. Again, what is it?

Roethke's "infinity," the "white light" and "windy cliffs" are configured squarely in the center of every poetic impulse the human being has probably ever felt. These phrases come from an orientation that is of starlight and horizons, nomadic wandering and intellectual exasperation, desperate love, inner delving, the desire to become immortal and then die softly. Mozart at the height of his "Requiem."

This desire to live forever in diverse guises—music, art, plant, animal, mountain top, coral reef, cloud, star—consumes everything about me. I was born with the impulse, I will die with the impulse, and, at death, nothing will have changed. In an instant, the once bright flame will have become embers. Centuries will have elapsed. I will have never existed. Perhaps paper, books, pen and ink will have long ceased to be a medium for the exchange of ideas. No remains whatsoever. And everyone I knew and loved will have also vanished.

Against these implacable odds, 10 trillion other organisms will have come into being and witnessed similar dissolutions.

Where, then, is the immortal mind?

"Thick and green the cypress, heedless of the frost, Soaked with dew the mushroom, suffering in the wind. What does a happy life amount to after all? I am not troubled by its brevity," wrote the 5th century poet, Hsieh Ling-Yun.[4]

He was one of the founders of the Shan-Shui (mountain/river) school of poetry, a subtlety of intuition and embrace that would ultimately evolve into the Chinese pictorial renaissance of the Northern and Southern Sung Dynasties. That expression, advanced by Hsieh, and later by the 10th and 11th century painters Li Ch'eng and Kuo Hsi, evoked an atmospheric indistinctness and a choice of imaginative locations suitable to an individual's reincarnation. The choice, as John Muir himself recognized, is a personal one. As the body courses its path, the mind re-formulates each footstep. It is physique and it is contemplation, both. It is the yin and the yang, energies directed into the Earth and up toward the heavens; angels ascending and descending Jacob's Ladder; thoughts arising in solitude and returning there. A transport of deliberate visualization that is so concentrated, so acutely formulated, as to ensure continuity in loss; biological transition back into the Earth after death.

This was the ancient Greek concept of Gaia, of a Mother Earth who gave all and received all. Does it mean that one can visualize one's death? I believe so. Down to the precise coordinates. If it is your intention to become a redwood seedling in the next life, then obviously one had better arrange for one's corpse, or its ashes, to be laid to rest in a redwood grove. Spread out as food for Karakoram snow leopards, or tidbits for the Sooty Albatross along the grassy knolls of Antarctica's Western Peninsula. Left mangled and exposed for the insects of some hanging garden in Polynesia. Or quietly nibbled away by hordes of multi-colored Angel fish along the cavernous shallows of the Australian Great Barrier Reef. Wherever you intend to spring up, go there. Go beneath a waterfall in the Arun Valley or near a quiet meadow in George Inness country. In your mind, as in real life. This has been my own delectation since childhood, a salvation that keeps rearing up with inviolate logic. For the prisoner behind bars, or the prisoner of his senses; for the medically incapacitated, the blind, the immobile—this dream of nature nevertheless obtains.

But the possibilities for rebirth—the planet's ceaseless *samsara*, its giving and taking, churning and recapitulating—go beyond mere practical matters of biological immortality, which I believe are self-evident. The solitudal vision of which I speak suggests the pertinacity of an individual's soul. Biology will never conquer the soul nor expunge it from the record of spiritual activity on Earth. We spend our lives learning, accumulating insight, gaining at least a modicum of sure-footedness. For what? To be cut down at the height of our wisdom? I don't think so. There is an ecological law of efficiency, thermodynamics, which would contradict so wasteful a tendency. Every cliché about nature indicates a patterned precision. Scientists are fond of pointing out that 98 percent of all sunlight appears to be wasted. That the green plants utilize a minute amount to perform their rambunctious photosynthetic duties. What do scientists think happens to the remaining bulk of sunlight? They don't know. Maybe, they surmise vaguely, it is reflected back into the atmosphere (the albedo) where it warms up the troposphere, triggers countless chemical reactions or dissipates into other useful forms of energy that drive the weather, the ocean currents, the hydrological cycle on Earth.

In other words, nothing is wasted. So why presume that the cosmos would waste the accumulated philosophy of an old man, of over 100 billion old men and women that have thus far graced this planet? It makes absolutely no sense.

An ecological awareness of this immortality factor means that a tropical rainforest, a mangrove, an Arctic vista, the prairies beyond the Urals and the deep marine waters of the Indian Ocean all abound with souls that have either deliberately or randomly become one another; leaves and kelp and every imaginable tooth and claw and speculai of biomass; eyes and brains and hearts and arms; ladybugs and eagles; zebras and poets. This dizzying life game has been going on relentlessly for over four billion years, promises to continue for another four billion years and is totally steeped in souls. Souls that speak as spirits and ghosts and fond hints of the everlasting.

To meditate on these matters, from a high cliff or a cozy futon, from a temple in India or a cave in the Sinai, has one important advantage: an individual has a choice. We may be unable to predict the moment or circumstances of our physical end, but we can certainly discipline our thoughts in advance, sketch our landing place, even formulate the interior design, the garden plot, the scenery and company of strangers and books and music into whose rousing orchestra we intend to take our place, which is what such meditation is ultimately about. There is an undeniable pleasure, or strength, in the foreknowledge that one is destined to come back as an albatross, or a snow leopard, if one so desires. The firm confidence that we are destined to enjoy the full pageant of biology in all its guises. Our spiritual evolution has engendered in us this self-conscious scenario, this imaginative possibility.

There are other practical benefits to such introspection, in this life, which are neither smitten with other worlds nor fatalistic. Perhaps it is the most obvious reason to study nature; to ponder its many incalculable messages. Not to do so is to ignore express telegrams which the Earth delivers to us every day; not to do so is to sleep complacently, to dismiss those precious gifts of which our life consists. The deep consideration of nature in us, all around us, is the expansion of our Being, of our capacity for love, for vision, for dreaming; for understanding what it is that allows us to breathe, to drink, to enjoy. All those things which we are about. The private vagaries of desire and hope, in the palm of our mind. And that is where this meditation begins and ends and begins again.

[1] Buddha's last words, in *The Wisdom of Buddhism*, edited by Christmas Humphreys, p. 94, New York: Random House, 1961.

[2] In Carsun Chang's *The Development of Neo-Confucian Thought*, Bookman Associates, New York, 1957, p. 350.

[3] "Meditative Sequences" quoted in *Contemplation and The Creative Process*, by Ann T. Foster, p. 102, The Edwin Mellen Press, 1985.

[4] Quoted in J. D. Frodsham, *The Murmuring Stream*, 2 volumes, University of Malaya Press, Kuala Lumpur, 1967.

XV
Viennese Ducks

Wrath is a short madnesse; madnesse is the murderer of reason;
so that anger transformes a man into a brute beast.
Give us therefore courage
(O Lord) to fight against this strong enemy…

—Thomas Dekker,
from *Foure Birds of Noahs Arke*[1]

It is well worth contemplating the world of ducks. The quack, *I have found, is the quintessential spark of conscience, the world's true voice. The quack, and the forces compelling it, are among the closest approximations I know to the joy of God.*

The contemplation of ducks (*Anatidae*) is a good thing, like listening to Vivaldi in the morning, taking a shower in a waterfall or lying naked in a moss garden, inviting ants and worms and caterpillars to crawl over oneself, feeling their little legs caressing the skin on long-distance errands whose beginning and end is no less mysterious than the stars. All in a garden, where life probably began.

There is a very special garden, the Stadtpark in the Vienna, that I love. Johann Strauss used to give concerts there. His gilded statue commemorates that fact and disciples continue to play music amid this grassy haven in the middle of the city where a series of ponds provides the livelihood for several hundred wonderful ducks, ravens, sparrows and pigeons who make a considerable concert themselves.

Ironically, the park is situated across the street from OPEC's headquarters. Ironic only because ducks—like water itself—do not mix with oil.

I feed the birds every day that I'm in town. It is a religion with me. First thing, to the local market where I buy a few loaves of bread and a box of cereal. Then, to the lake.

The various birds know when I'm coming. They descend like a locust swarm onto my park bench, compete for standing space on my head and shoulders. I like it. In fact, I've gotten to know some of the birds very intimately. We haven't exchanged cards or anything, but we have become close friends.

How innocent ducks are, preening and plucking and paddling amidst their wild gregarious communes, green heads, chestnut breasts, purplish-blue borders, white tails, colorful flanks, rab-rab-rabs and quack-wack-wacks, a continuous festivity that has ignored the Anschluss, the bombs, Hitler and the Austrian diet, which is big on duckling.

A duck is a magnificent being, its feathers radiating the brightest or the subtlest of hues. There is nothing in their character, nothing at all, to detract from the affection they must elicit. Are there duck wars? Duck murders? I doubt it. What duck disputes I've noticed—fueled by hunger, or territorial need—tend only to re-affirm the down-to-earth or Gandhian aesthetic that defines their assorted interactions.

To be nibbled by a duck, to lend an ear to their amateurish outrages, is to encounter on Earth an anatomy incapable of hostility. Deer and bunnies compete in this passivity, but ducks typically exceed these cousins by en-dearing themselves with that extra measure of intrepid curiosity normally lacking among most other creatures. That this penchant for approaching humans should merely stem from constant hunger for bread only furthers the opinion—formed over centuries—that in ducks, as in the lakes and marshes and estuaries they have claimed, is to be found the purest philoso-phy of pragmatism and non-violence on the planet.

To what use can such philosophy be applied? Surely the crisis in Ireland, South Africa, the Balkan states or the Middle East?

Without a doubt, the peaceful world of duckdom has its own unwritten treaties, genetic maps and conflict resolutions that are universal, even in the marshes of the Tigris-Euphrates, where some believe ducks originated. The business of ducks might well be construed as the business of America, of all nations, even the OPEC ones. Putting bread on every duck's table. Educating the young. Instilling in them duck values of family, social responsibility, moral fiber. Ducks are free thinkers, pro-choice, pro-privacy. They are not shy about competing in the global marketplace, however, as witnessed by their zealous bread hunting expeditions in the vicinity of the park bench from which I frequently toss those whole wheat loaves like a candidate running for office. I would gladly run for any office the ducks suggested.

Among ducks there is no capital punishment. And while revenge is not unheard of, and ducks are certainly known to pursue one another in a fury, sometimes for as long as a minute, the result is never more than a few puffed-up feathers and quiet irritation. Never a drop of blood.

Ducks take care of their old, who often lounge on the grass as couples or old friends. Seeing them together, musing on the great imponderables, I cannot help but reflect on the sublime.

None of this is meant to overstate the obvious: ducks rear up, fan their buns, take off, always astutely alive, in a mad medley of care-free intention, the whole world their duck grass. A royal bird given neither to excess nor fanatical display, as far as I have witnessed, there is a quiet discretion among ducks that reminds me of Charlie Chaplin at his best—when poignancy and zeal were fused in the moment. Or what I imagine to have been the gentleness of Christ. It may be their reason for being, after all the quacking has died down; a princely calm which is their heritage. The twilight on lake water, so still, so infinitely in tune with the original stillness on the original lake of the aboriginal Earth. Going back into time to the first elation, or quack, of God.

So, it's well worth meditating on ducks.

1 From *Foure Birds of Noahs Arke*, by Thomas Dekker, 1609, New York: D. Appleton & Co., 1925.

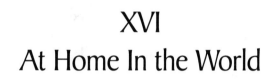

XVI
At Home In the World

'The wolf and the lamb shall feed together.'

—Isaiah 65:25

In the company of grizzly bears, or the mental enigma which brown bears pose—the universal quotient of risk, uncertainty, defenselessness—one is able to better cherish our fragility, and ultimately, with a little effort, to make friends with strangers. This is the only hope of lasting peace. The effort begins in mind, where terror is so superficially lodged.

The southeastern Alaskan night was fast closing in as I traversed to the far mid-section of a steep slope of rock and alders. A mile back, a few of my friends were crawling into sleeping bags and noshing on their night snacks, reclining along a rocky inlet that led to the Grand Pacific Ice Cap we'd come to explore. Above the ice, directly before me, Mt. Fairweather rose sheer into the stars.

The previous week had seen no rain, only blistering sun, and the creeks, ordinarily slow to start, were coming down side canyons as torrents. I had assumed the task of scouting the coming day's route and presently approached one such river, understood by the pitch of its roar and the evidential weight of boulders tossed along its current, the sound of ice floes breaking up in late spring.

I craned around the knife-edged ridge but was unable to actually see the descending side gorge. Spread-eagled, 200 feet above the inlet—an eight-mile wide fjord, cloaked in rock and moss and verdant thicket, and up which the infrequent cruise ships ventured to show off the calving ice to their occupants—I squirmed back away from the lip. The river's blast was all around me. But I heard something else, too, which sounded like a snort. I looked down between my legs.

And there, not ten feet below, were two dark shades, moving: a grizzly bear sow and her cub. Perhaps 1500 pounds between them. On a ledge, sure-pawed, perhaps sleepy, rummaging dexteriously for berries. Tai Chi masters of the twilight. I froze. There is that old rule of thumb: if you should ever have the bad luck to surprise a grizzly bear with her newborn, say good-bye to the world.

The Japanese moon, a sweeping aurora borealis, lazy distant cusps of mist over the burgundy-red waters of the fjord, all struck me in the same instant as especially perfect. Tears were involuntarily streaming down my face. My body was shaking. The loud coursing of blood in my veins was adding to the fulmination of the river. I could go on about the physiological changes that came over me just then. I assume they are universal harbingers of disaster. The stillness of birds before an earthquake. The coiling of a cornered snake, like a harmonic series of tones, premonitory guides to surrender. My life was over.

But let me preface this incident which, I should add, the author of these pensées did not survive, or not in the usual sense, to talk about.

As far back as Zeno in the 4th century B.C., the concept of global citizenry was well established among the Stoics. That's very important, under such circumstances.

"No man is an island, entire of itself," John Donne later wrote. "Every man is a piece of the continent, a part of the main. If a clod be washed away by the sea, Europe is the less, as well as if a promontory were, as well as if a manor of thy friends or of thine own were. Any man's death diminishes me, because I am involved in mankind; and therefore never send to know for whom the bell tolls—it tolls for thee."[1]

In the latter part of the 17th century, men like John Ray[2] and William Derham[3] responded to the poetry of John Donne with a scientific call for the unity of nature. Summarizing a feverish century of physics, geology and biology, Ray and Derham merged the sciences with theology, an outcome which claimed that all of God's diverse creation was interrelated.[4] And furthermore, that, such manifestations could be claimed to be the best of all possible worlds. In Alexander Pope's phrase, "whatever is, is right…All are but parts of one stupendous whole, Whose body Nature is, and God the soul."[5] And while God was abandoned by increasing droves 200 years later, one still had his ecological web of life as proof of…*something*, which has been our obsession ever since.

That surrender has become increasingly uninteresting, partly I suspect because we have assimilated so much information about Him. We think we know a thing or two. And our knowledge no longer warrants belief in the unknown. If it's unknown, one need simply find out about it, whether it be the aerodynamics of a dragonfly or the permafrost of Mars. No need to call it a Divinity. And this provision has guaranteed a level of hubris that is not easily shaken, for it is connate with a Faith in Ourselves, one more Americanism, instinct with the frontier, and every individual his right to be himself, to bear arms, etc. God, if not dead, has been demystified. But what remains after all is said, twisted and dismissed, is the loveliness that surrounds God, and which the human organism immemorially requires.

There is, then, a second history of this hubris that has fostered the renunciation of the unknown and the celebration of the self. Call it the "me generation," the economic prioritists, the infinite resource school, the techno-salvationists who are convinced that Japan is the enemy and life's greatest gifts measurable on Wall Street. These are the burn-outs, cancer and heart attack prone, meat-eaters, fast drivers, eyes fixed upon some heaven usually behind glass, twenty, thirty, eighty stories up. Supreme narcissists, "whatever works" is their vacuous right-of-passage. In other words, me, myself and I.

The neuroses which attend such progress are swept forward by delusions of detail and scintillating truisms.

But, of course, there is third level of experience, not half as cynical or hell-bent, and that is the vast range of spiritual longings that most people share; the ordinary yearning by which individuals actually live, neither lost behind blinders, nor out destroying rainbows with sheer science. And for them, there is eternal mystery which envelops nearly every question of any significance.

The one that most perplexes me, the three-pronged query raised by Gauguin so innocently beneath one of his larger canvases, is simply put, Why I am here? What is the purpose of this universe? How are we to get through the day? That's not exactly how Gauguin phrased it, but close enough, and frankly, pinioned up above that bear, I was not at leisure to paraphrase precisely.

But those were the great existential sighs that ached in my throat. The surrender to God? Are you there? I asked. Is someone out there? The acceptance of Beauty? The notion that nothing in nature is done in vain, but that all is vanity? I was marooned by these ecclesiastical and semantic contradictions. Because what they really amounted to was my verifiable demise. And the stars of that implacable heaven would shine as brightly, not more darkly; and His inscrutable gaze would stare upon the scene, one more predation, and commend the feeding of a cub. Life is good, the bear would belch in the coming days, feasting on my more delicate left-overs up on that ledge. And what of me? Had I the right to carp and grovel over matters as picayunish as mere destiny?

We are all one. That was the lesson of the poets and philosophers in centuries past. Nature, man, woman, every animal species—one.

One what?

The notion of actually becoming one with that bear—of being eaten alive, in other words—held meager consolation in the Alaskan twilight. It is well and good to rhapsodize such collision courses of philosophy, safely removed by years and miles. But those moments of greatest risk were horrifying.

Still, I would not have missed them for the world, considering what then transpired.

I could not move to the left, the knife-edge. Nor was I able to climb above, where mixed terrain gave way to steep granite slabs. My only chance was to retrace my way across the series of ledges and trust that the bears would not notice me. Despite my utter chaos of fear, the sense that there was absolutely no hope, I nevertheless mustered faith; I confronted my own death, as they say, as 60 million human beings say every year, and hundreds of millions of other organisms cry out every day, each minute, millennium after millennium.

The very first move and to my astonishment, my bad luck, I managed to dislodge a rock which shot out and smacked right into the sow's large shoulders.

It began.

I had to look, to stop and examine the impact of my ungainliness. Did she think me a crazed mountain goat? Did she presume me a predator? Or did she see...me? Had she ever before seen a human being, a bipedally strange creature, obviously unafraid? She roared, while the cub started to cry, human baby-like. And as she roared, she reared up against the cliff, her front paws reaching eight, nine feet up at me. The right paw slashed out, a rapid fire movement, but I saw it slowly—a paw the size of a large non-vegetarian pizza—that missed me by mere inches. And as she strained to get me, I fled to the right. Stumbling in a dervishly amphetamized stampede of grotesque adverbs on the run across that darkened wall. And she came after me. An adult grizzly bear can run 40 miles an hour uphill. Downhill it has slightly less agility, probably worth 5 miles an hour, which gave me perhaps four seconds of life, at best.

I mentioned Zeno and the Stoics for a reason. Not simply because of their stoicism—which to coin Byron's poem "Manfred" makes it one's fatality to live—but because they evidently believed in a global commons, a deep ecological sense of camaraderie on Earth. The Greeks and Ionians, like their subsequent Renaissance disciples, advocated a daily commerce with the gods of nature. Aristotle wrote volume after volume on the subject of animals, marvelling at their similarities to men. And there have since been any number of inspired peace plans, utopias, gardens of delight—inspired by Hugo Grotius, Rubens, Brueghel, Sannazaro, Sir Thomas More, Campanella, etc.—that perceived biodiversity as the highest form of morality, a law unto itself to which all human prudence and legislation must aspire. The Northern Sung Chinese, the 16th century Italians and 17th century Dutch and Flemish, the Safavid Persians and Indian Guptas all painted animal nature as part of the common heritage, a living fraternity of impulses no less important than our own.

To recall our philosophical upbringing according to these harmonious urgings—the I-Thou which must inhere between every neurological assemblage, even between combative cells and squirming follicle mites—is the spiritual in *Homo sapiens*. When one considers Gandhi in the context of biology, there is fierce debate, of course. The common sense conservatism holds that any theology of pacifism has already collapsed into mere fairy tale long before the pre-Cambrian; that the record of zoology on Earth, which is largely the product of single-minded prokaryotes and eukaryotes, is consumed by violence of one form or another. That the consumption of one organism by another, and that rich assortment of violent tendencies that have been allegedly inherited by so-called higher life forms, is basic to all the first genes and genetic crystals across the planet. Moreover, that life, as Hobbes so bluntly stated, is nothing more than the struggle to survive.

Darwin, often wrongly quoted, pointed out that survival is not what our life is about; but that evolution is the point of it all. If it were merely survival we would have all remained in the Icelandic mud baths, or as perfect sharks coursing the pellagic abyss for 100 million years.

It may well be that all the first lessons of science, once partly right, have lost their relevance, simply fade out of vogue and are eventually forgotten. We must remember that science is not some collective truth that exists outside of scientists; anymore than economics, or politics or even the mathematical conception of "zero" has any reality whatsoever, but for the men and women who theorized these fancy-dressings, and their many students and colleagues who then elevated them to supposed "fact."

The world is not a place of facts, but of unquenchable enigma, utter beauty, beauty without particular name or reason; no providential superintendent nor demonic catcaller; rather, a vast dance spreading across darkness, lit by forces which have no outside looking in. Our only clue to its reality, this firmament of life, is our own bleating in the night, warm words, groping touch, childish games and grown-up joys. In other words, affinity with one another, with everything, even with the bear, what the Greeks termed *physiolatry*, the love of nature; and what others, like the human geographer

Yi-Fu Tuan have aptly hailed "*topophilia,*" or Edward Wilson, "*biophilia.*"

Enough linguistics.

I didn't look back. I felt her charging breath and mammoth mass bearing down on me with the ferocity of primeval times. I've heard from others that brown bears often chase down their human prey, only for fun. There was a woman hiker who ran thousands of feet, the grizzly right behind her, easily able to have struck her down with a single swipe of its paw, but it never did. Rather, according to an eyewitness, the bear literally played with her (the woman was in no mental state to recognize the game) and when she collapsed, unconscious, the bear sniffed her, looked around and left.

That was no sow with cub, however. And I should also point out that weeks before, a ranger down in Gustavus had begged me to carry a gun, which I refused. It seems that a year or so before a soloist had been dropped off along the same 20 mile stretch by float plane. His body was never found, but his camera was, uneaten, with which he had courageously, or naively, recorded the attack of a grizzly down to the last 40 or so feet, image after image. He never managed to click the button after 40 feet, which—at a full gallop—would take the bear less then a second to cross. There's just no predicting. No science that can say.

My own seconds were closing in. I felt the coming lunge the way a lightning bolt bursts the bubble of air before it, announcing its immanent explosion. I was already one foot into the grave, the blood in my throat hardly held down, my eyes blurred with transmigration. The same quality I imagine as that of a plane crash, its victims suspended between heart attack and the total detonation of Earth, fast closing in.

When my only chance, a spectacular possibility, blossomed right there to my side—the cliff!

In the near darkness I could fool myself that the high conical mound of soft detritus was just 10, maybe 20 feet below. I did not consider that it was in fact closer to 20 *stories*, 200 vertical feet; that there were bound to be outcrops, bumps in the night; that more than likely I would be dashed, then eaten.

But I hadn't the luxury of considering these graphic options, for within milliseconds, the bear was upon me, its furry mass essentially sliding into first base, careening with just enough hesitancy—due to the cliff—to spare me the actual pile-up.

And I was gone, free, out into space.

Have you ever fallen in the night? Say, off a cliff into the ocean? Even from a hayloft into a rick on ground level? Well, it is probably the most absolving venture the body can initiate.

I've floated for days, in truth—ever since. I still have not landed, though the science of a fall can be calculated easily enough.

The darkness caressed my face, granted me the wings of an angel, and I flew like Peter Pan across glacial moraine and ancient valley; flipped over that pile of rocky debris below the cliff like a circus clown, my hip slashed open, nothing very serious, my butt bruised, and kept flying. The bear, discomfitured by my sudden disappearance, roared once again, then all at once appeared in the fjord, swimming methodically in my same direction, determined to cut me off.

I flew across the kelp strewn rocks in the dark, flopping face down, spraining ankles, bashing hands, more alive to the ecstasies of my body than ever before.

In the distance I saw my friends. I tried to scream, to warn them, but no voice came forth. Was I dead?

My ghost finally reached camp, though by then they had seen the bear coming behind me and fled uphill, dragging their sleeping bags behind them. The food was sprawled across the beach-head. I was crumpled down now, alone, 20 seconds ahead of the sow and her devoted little cub that had managed to keep up.

The bears stopped. Fifty feet away from me, and squinted at camp, sniffing the night air, then gingerly vanished into the thickets.

I eventually fell asleep.

For the next month I lived with those bears, always leaving my food outside my tent. Often they would come in the afternoon, smell the food, pee near the zipped-up entrance, make a certain merriment, then head off.

Once, while crossing a river, stopped in the middle sandbar, I noticed the sow and her cub on the other side, not 30 feet away across a waist-deep rushing tributary. They recognized me. We stared at one another for a good three minutes, this time I didn't run, the cub playing with a butterfly in the air on the edge of the white water, then they moved on.

On my last day in the region, returning from a multi-day climb across heavily crevassed glaciers, I descended into the mudflats of the Grand Pacific icecap, and there witnessed a set of paw prints heading out into the fjord, prints roughly twice the size and depth of the sow's, which I had come to know well. It must have been her mate, an 1800 pound male who never showed his face. He was a phantom, though there were nights when I'm sure he had visited my tent; just as there have been countless other nights since then, when I have visited his. For the wolf and the lamb have slept side by side in this unpredictable, perfect world.

"You like naturalness so much. I think you cling to it, it is not natural anymore.…When our mind is perfectly free and open to everything—like a mirror—it is natural mind."[6]

[1]John Donne, "Devotion XVII," 1624, in *The Complete Poetry and Selected Prose of John Donne & The Complete Poetry of William Blake*, p. 332, Modern Library, New York, 1946.
[2]*The Wisdom of God Manifested in the Works of the Creation*, 12th ed., London: John Rivington, John Ward, Joseph Richardson, 1759.
[3]William Derham, *Physico-Theology: or, A Demonstration of the Being and Attributes of God, from His Works of Creation*, 2 vols., New ed., London: Printed for A. Strahan, et al., 1798.
[4]See Clarence Glacken's fascinating analysis of these two men and their era in his definitive, *Traces on the Rhodian Shore - Nature And Culture In Western Thought From Ancient Times To The End Of The Eighteenth Century*, pp. 415-428, University of California Press, Berkeley, 1967.
[5]ibid., quoted from *Essay on Man*, Ep. I, x & ix, p. 522.
[6]Suzuki Roshi, in *The Science of Being and the Art of Living*, by Jacob Needleman, p. 56, Doubleday & Co., New York, 1970.

XVII
Environmental Meditation

You go, my son,
Go to the great courtyard.
Don't let the horse go ahead of you.
Give the horse some food.
Stop and feed him well…
You will arrive, my son, in a white room.
Don't stand, my child, under the icons,
Stand, my child, instead among the fields
And bow to them like a lord.

—from *Mother Russia—The Feminine Myth in Russian Culture*
by Joanna Hubbs[1]

In this final meditation, I follow the biodiversity of thought. Thought which is a champion and mirror of nature. Nature whose only goal is the perpetual celebration of itself. The complete, unstinting joy of being. Just being. There is no greater solace.

C*onatus* is defined as a "natural tendency." Philosophers think of it as a mysterious, all-encompassing desire in human animals to be what they can possibly be; that force in the rest of nature which animates inertia, and self-realizes the animate. As a 17th century Dutch ethical principle, formulated most elegantly in the works of Benedict Spinoza[2], this sense of a universal impulse or aliveness ensures and perpetuates every possible miracle that meditation can ever hope to achieve. Meditation and *conatus* are, in fact, synonymous.

The human desire, the natural force: two impulses in the cosmos. The desire is enveloped by the greater force, as one would logically expect. I don't know—do you?—whether there is a need of *conatus* in other organisms, which dispense with name calling and personal motivation, with self-help or neurotic obsession: they simply ARE.

Simply ARE. How to *simply BE*? Could I bear it? Would it be boring, would it be grand? To be a natural force? My limitations are precise, even pleasurable: I see the extent of my arms and fingers, my toes and marginal peripheral vision. My grip is just so tight, my heart beats just so many times per minute. The dogs outrun me, the birds, needless to say, outfly me. Even the humblest bugs outcrawl me. The sea cares nothing for me. This ME is a liability, a disaster, and yet, without it, my voice is disembodied, a genetic wisp of cloud without a home, or a purpose. The sky, a mere idea. I do not know where the wind is going or what the seasons are thinking. I have tried to forget myself in the vain hope of learning the language of albatross. Certain sages said it was possible.

The albatross were the ones, after all, who first discovered that the Earth was round, flying tens of thousands of miles high in the heavens, all winter long, bearing the Antarctic inclement blizzards with the equanimity of a single, burning thought: springtime! No different than the perennial which patiently awaits its renewal.

How unlike the me in me that has entangled itself in a flotsam of hurried hopes and introspective *conatus*. Sorting out the world-as-contradiction. Stemming the chasm of ideas, probing into the darkness of myself without equipment or map. Will I one day re-emerge on the surface, like a dog from a lake, and shake off these many impediments to simply being?

Then again, how can I be sure that the world really is contradictory? That what I take to be my limitations, the conflict all around me, the dilemmas, traumas, catastrophes, as well as the possibilities for love, for joy, for beauty, are really nothing more than "simply being?" The smooth confluence of sub-atomic particles?

A tantalizing conjunction, bound by two words, eleven letters and a space. "Simply being"…Formed by language, by the vastly complex social-ization, both self-willed and unself-willed, by the grammar of centuries, the deep structure of millennia, by 100 billion human lives, consumed by human history; two words, the by-product of reaction times, personality quirks, by special circumstances—no bloated belly, no gun aimed at my head—by this phase in my life that allows me to ponder such proverbial fairies on my pinhead in the first place.

In other words, "simply are" is not so simple.

I am humbled by the two words, driven to appreciate everything good in this universe. All the philosophy in the world, in the end, comes down to these words. The Jains said so several thousand years ago: "Let things simply be as they are!" This was Mahavira's message. The same clairvoyant child's logic infuses Vermeer and Marcus Aurelius. Prayers from every culture and period of history convey an identical native wisdom.

As sculptors of our own lives, we take the Earth clay of our bodies, shape it to our pleasure, loose its shape in the thick of our distractions, bake it according to our individual tastes, and crack up as an inevitable result of planetary, even stellar forces over which our personalities and habits have little control.

Contradiction or the Tao? Or both?

Both.

The world contains it all. The *me* seizes upon details because I am of details, my limitations are details. At the same time, the ecological being points the way towards ideals—a philosophy of life, a particular painting, a mountain—and renders metaphors that summarize volition, the exotic-sounding body of water within myself. Today it is a polluted Hudson River. Tomorrow, the Antarctic Ocean.

Detailed and plodding, my contradictory confluence of thoughts appropriates pleasurable notions and sensory stimuli and within seconds engineers a concept. The concept, in turn, accumulates into a dream, a goal. The goal of a lifetime, perhaps; or a religious belief, or a conviction worth dying for. And all stemming from a sudden light across the land, through the window, the dreamy singing of sparrows across the street from a church, the furrowed sadness in the once unsullied face of a person we loved. Whatever the instant, it has grown, now, into a burning dedication. Existential. Self-aware. Matured. And it came from a detail in the world.

Details and vast dreams. Solid substance and high-flying deities. I live thinking between these two extremes. Immersed in an aesthetic, meditational steady-state. This is my survival. I must survive, and I must combat habituation to do so, lest I become as insensitive as the evening news which so facilely glosses over calamity; as mechanical as the morning paper that recently reported on 300 Liberians chopped up into little pieces.

What are the properties of habituation? How do I break the spell that has addicted so many fathomless generations within me? This civilizing sensation—that's all it is, really—which coddles the head so that one's ideas are scarcely one's own; one's family merely genetic markers in the long anadromous rush upstream. I've seen the salmon do it, not one, but hundreds of thousands, commingling frantically. Who are they? Are they individuals? Am I an individual? Are these thoughts mere echoes from across the canyon where we were all born?

Spawning behavior, habituation, distant echoes, genetic connections, ideas that have been voiced in other disguises, all those that have cried, smiled, laughed before me; my parents, my brother, my friends, my other animal companions, the views, the windows before which I have stood and gazed out, the foods I eat, the clothes I wear, or lack of clothes, my hours of sleep, my hours during the day. All these things in mind.

Squinting after clearer vision: beyond this stasis, this glass of wine, a glint of fire, a touch of love, the murmuring heart. Craving restlessly to power through the strangleholds of the familiar. Into the unknown?

How can I be sure that I am addicted? There are certain moments when I am absolutely certain that I have been in a deep sleep of custom, comfort and self-control. When did I begin taking this drug? When did my parents and their parents get hooked within the secure mental borders? On a shtetl in Russia? In a cave, 10,000 years ago, along that old Cimarron River in New Mexico, where the Folsom arrowheads were discovered among a herd of fossilized bison? My ancestors. Flint chippers?

Or further back, this habituation: a Ground Sloth from the post-Pleistocene? A thirsty pig deer? An Upper Triassic vertebrate from Arizona, nameless, purposeless? A *Cosmonautilus dilleri* from deep in the Indian Ocean? Who was I? A slender-limbed reptile? A free-swimming Crinoid? A small fish? A graptolite with water wings? A pebble of the Algonkian?

I do not know where the habituation began, where I came from or where I'm going. But during those special moments when the air in my nostrils tastes of liberation, I sense the possibility of delirious disappearance, of some outrageous destiny or pleasure in the beyond, right here, right over there, right now!

Not knowing the full extent of this passion, the involuntary musculature or adrenalin of its intoxications, I have left careful instructions for my wife with regard to my death, my "practical immortality," or, as stated above, my disappearance. Part of me is to be dropped into a deep blue yawning crevasse along the Antarctic peninsula. Another portion dropped from 30,000 feet into the waters of French Polynesia. And still another part buried in a mossy cave high in northern Arunachal Pradesh, beneath a certain waterfall. I'd like a testicle jettisoned into outer space in the direction of nowhere, and my hair cast over Angel Falls. I'd like my nose left in the kitchen of a certain Parisian restaurant I know and my fingers plopped into an alkaline mud bath, 162 degrees, in central Iceland. I'd certainly want some of my blood smeared here and there—on the white streaks of granite up along the east side of El Capitan, at the Bahubali cave of Ellora, on some old brick in Delft, on the stone oracle at Delphi. And some skin samples planted in the highlands of Bora Bora, in a patch of moss at Ryoan-ji, along the Tar Inlet of Glacier Bay. And I'd want my lips and brain and eyes buried conventionally, deep in the soil, beside my mate, wherever that may be. There is a Kurdish saying, "Everything is forgiven the brave."

Can I possibly desire what is impossible to control? Death will take us, soon enough. Enjoy the control while it lasts, my mind scolds me. It is merely today's frustration that bids me to let go, to cast off this anchor in traditional consciousness and set sail into the new life I imagine awaits me, right there!

And yet, it *is* right there! That kingdom of clarities and promise, of evolutionary felicities which "simply are."

Are they more than the mountain? The sea? The love and need in a child's gaze? Can there be a kingdom more responsive, more sensitive, any more beautiful and perfect than what simply is?

Why do I push myself always, ceaselessly, inexpertly Beyond?

Beyond perfection?

No.

I push my thoughts, my gut, to come even remotely towards that perfection, here, now. I call it Beyond simply to delineate the *this* from the *that*. But I now know that these grandiose divisions, linguistic, conceptual, artistic, civil, scientific, mathematical, social, philosophical…are merely details of a unified effort—no theory, *effort*—towards re-unification, acceptance: myself, yourself, ourselves, Gandhi, the albatross, this many-wedded soul, at peace, in unison. And it is good. It is gentle. It is beautiful.

How do I solidify what is, again, mere doctrine? By what means might I transform the pedantry of soul-searching, into soul? The desire to be artistic into art? The love of nature into nature? The love of people into people? The love of anything into pure love, unconditional, unspecified?

Whether the homeless are mentally disabled, simply down on their luck or the victims of a hurricane, we are all homeless, in the end. Homeless, but world-full.

And in this world-fullness is a mind capable of attaining its own, mind-full possibilities. Of sowing its clover and achieving its ancient rapport. Of moving from mind into heart and from heart into the whole world.

But how, how is it done, the mind demands? On a planet rife with contradiction, paradox, hatred, the unfairness of shortfall, of losing when others seem to be gaining?

The heart knows the answer, gracefully or sloppily, with any number of salvations and attritions, with regrets and adamant smiles. Never losing sight of the goal. Of the fire that burns in the human soul.

Mark my word, that soul exists. It is no illusion. It is imperishable just as Nature is imperishable. They are synonymous truths that have struck an eternal concord in the fiery furnaces of light that has not yet even reached the Earth. Light that is no feeble consolation in the dark, but the paintbrush of evolution, guided not by cosmic dusts and hallowed names, but by individuals struggling to be good, to measure up to the proportions and soundness and exquisitely true blue nature of nature, all of its great and small and mind-full creatures—rock, ant, glacier, rainforest—which simply…are!

Every day, in the consoling privacy of this idea of Nature, I take the time to stop whatever else I'm doing and re-formulate my entire evolution according to its urgings. A sweet, imperfect, humbling meditation. A symphony of musical thought, and every organism on Earth a part of the concert.

No blind faith, but the common sense of kindness, beauty, peace. To walk softly. To grant the convenant of trust and dignity to all things, which I would grant to myself, regardless of my limitations, my shortcomings. To know that my inner nature, and the Nature that surrounds me, are whistling the same tune—in the city, beside cemeteries, out in the country, on the mountain top, in all the blades of grass, on the currents of every wind, in each rain drop, acid or otherwise, in all the paintings and poems and satoris, about every wild brain, vein and cell; even in the center of the atom. This same meditation, in one form or another gives me the hope to keep going.

[1] *Mother Russia—The Feminine Myth in Russian Culture*, by Joanna Hubbs, p. 82, Indiana University Press, Bloomington, 1988.
[2] See *Ethics*, by Spinoza, translated by R. H. M. Elwes, Dover Publishers, New York, 1951. See Freya Mathews' commentary on Spinoza in her book, *The Ecological Self*, Barnes & Noble Books, Maryland, 1991.

About the Author

Michael Tobias, former Assistant Professor of Humanities and Environmental Studies at Dartmouth College, is the author and editor of twenty works of fiction and non-fiction, as well as the writer, director and producer of over sixty films. Ecologist, historian, explorer and artist, Tobias has conducted research, directed films, written books, and climbed mountains on every continent. His works include *Rage & Reason*, *Life Force*, *Believe*, *Fatal Exposure*, *Mountain People*, *The Mountain Spirit*, and the best-seller, *Voice of the Planet*, upon which Tobias created his groundbreaking ten-hour television miniseries by the same title, which has been broadcast in over twenty countries.

If you enjoyed this book
you may be interested in our other offerings.
For a free Crossing Press catalog call,
toll-free, 800/777-1048.